BEE ENCOURAGED

Stories of Resilience by Black Sisters of Faith

Caretha F. Crawford

This book is dedicated to all Black women who have faced countless challenges throughout history. Despite the injustices of life, we are thankful for a Savior who grants us grace and favor. Together, we celebrate our resilience and the strength that unites us as we support one another.

Contents

Foreword

Dr. Caretha Crawford has done it once again!

With a gifted ear and a compassionate heart, she tunes in to the voices of women from many different backgrounds, allowing their stories to rise with truth and power. "BEE ENCOURAGED: *Stories of Resilience by Black Sisters of Faith*" is a testament to what unfolds when Black women speak openly about their journeys. The pain, the triumph, the healing, and the faith that carried them when life felt heavy, invisible, or overwhelming.

In these pages, Black women reveal the deep places of the soul where love and loss, protection and hurt, grief and healing, manipulation and survival intersect. Their honesty reminds us that our connection with God is critical. It is God who keeps us when we cannot keep ourselves. It is God who sees us when we feel invisible. It is God who holds us together when life attempts to pull us apart. Each story invites us to take off the mask, to breathe again, and to *Trust God* who walks with us, speaks to us, and guides us through every valley.

This book is more than a gathering of stories; it is a sacred space. A place where God's presence meets human vulnerability, where courage is honored, resilience is awakened, and faith is strengthened. As you turn each page and read each story, may you see God's hand at work, healing wounds, restoring hope, and transforming lives in ways only He can.

These stories remind us to *Trust God*, to hold on to our faith, and to never give up on the One who never gives up on us. May every testimony encourage your heart, deepen your faith, and affirm that God is still healing, still restoring, and still transforming His daughters today.

Peace & Blessings,
Reverend Sherlene McIntosh

Acknowledgments

Sharing personal details about one's life can be a vulnerable experience. It takes courage and strength to decide to open up, allowing others to learn from our pain and struggles. However, once we have healed and overcome our challenges, we often feel compelled to share our stories to encourage others. Scripture reminds us to "...encourage one another and build one another up..." (1 Thessalonians 5:11, NASB).

Reflecting on the challenges of my childhood and the current state of our world, especially in our nation, I felt a strong urge from God to write a book aimed at encouraging my Black sisters in the faith. I also felt the need to invite other sisters to share their stories of triumph. Sixteen Black women collaborated to create a powerful narrative of resilience and faith, which we are excited to present to you. As you read our stories, you may find that they resonate with your own experiences. Together, they provide testimony that God has gone ahead of every difficult and dangerous situation and has made the crooked paths straight.

Walk with these sixteen Black sisters or better, soar with them and BEE encouraged by their lived experiences.

Dr. Michelle Boone-Thornton, Selah retreats sister; **Lakia Bradley**, my mentee (BWIM), In Pursuit of His Presence Worship Arts (IPHP) graduate, and co-laborer in ministry; **Theresa Royal Brown,** a friend and colleague; **Beverly Claiborne,** a mentee, friend and co-laborer in ministry; **Dr. Caretha Franks Crawford,** publisher, editor and writer; **Pastor Pamela Franks**, cousin and co-laborer in ministry; **Robin Hinton,** BWIM sister;

Rhonda Lindo, cousin and dance minister; **Wanda M. Morris,** IPHP graduate; **Pastor Hewlette Pearson,** friend and colleague; **Rev. Dr. Marjorie Duncan Reed,** BWIM sister; **Judy Reid,** co-laborer; **Nicola Ross,** IPHP graduate; **Carolyn Simms,** college friend; **Tonya Swindell,** cousin; **Dr. Shryl Whigham,** IPHP graduate.

Special "Thank You"

Sherlene McIntosh, thank you are two small words that cannot fully express my gratitude. Please accept them as a token of my appreciation for writing the foreword to this book, which celebrates the resilience of remarkable Black women like you. Your own inspiring bounce-back stories could have easily been featured in this book. I am grateful for dear sisters like you. BEE Amazing!

Introduction

I chose the *BEE* as a symbol of encouragement for this book because of the misconception surrounding its ability to fly. Scientists and engineers once believed that BEES defied the odds when they took to the air, as their bodies and wings were thought to be disproportionate. According to earlier theories, the BEE'S body design made flying aerodynamically impossible, which became known as the BEE paradox. However, later studies revealed that BEE'S wings are designed for both thrust and lift, enabling them to fly. It wasn't until recently that even the most brilliant minds recognized that BEES were inherently designed for flight.

Much like the BEE, the innate potential of Black women to soar has often gone unnoticed, ignored, underestimated, disregarded or disputed.

Black women increasingly challenge the myth that we can't achieve great things. We are visionaries, creators, legacy builders, and pioneers, all while managing families and households. Black women have stepped into high-profile roles and are advancing in companies, industries, governments, schools, universities, churches, religious, and civic organizations. It is not that our intelligence and abilities aren't evident; often, we simply aren't recognized for our accomplishments. Have you noticed how our counterparts tend to wait for us to make a move, only to mimic it or take credit for our ideas without recognizing us as the original creators?

Consider this: if Black women were not designed to be strong, brilliant, and courageous, why does the opposition expend so many resources trying to hold us back? If we couldn't fly, why would they bother trying to clip our wings?

According to physics, BEES wings are flexible, allowing for twists and rotations during flight.

Black women are like BEES; in that we know how to pivot mid-course. We are resilient, akin to the punching bag toy that my children once played with in my classroom. This toy is weighted at the bottom, with air at the top. When struck with force, it leans backward but quickly bounces back. No amount of pressure can keep it down.

Black women possess incredible bounce-back power. Time and again, we face challenges—be it emotional, psychological, or physical—but we recover and push forward with renewed determination to succeed.

A study of the BEE community shows that while male BEES play a valuable role, it is the female BEES, known as worker BEES, who do the majority of the work. They produce and gather food, choose their leader (the queen BEE), and serve as protectors. Only females possess a stinger.

Throughout history, Black women have proven that we can produce, protect and soar. Countless Black women have left a legacy for us to follow.

Some contemporary Black women who are making a significant impact on the world include Michelle Obama, Kamala Harris, Jasmine Crockett, Ketanji Brown Jackson, Dr. Mae Jemison, Viola Davis, Simone Biles, Tamron Hall, Priscilla Shirer, CeCe Winans, and Rev. Dr. Suzan Johnson Cook (my mentor, The R.E.A.L. Black Women in Ministry Thrive Initiative). This is just a partial list; there are so many more deserving of recognition.

In my circle, there are extraordinary women who may not be famous but are thriving and making lasting impacts in their communities. You will meet some of them in this book and hear their stories of overcoming adversity. They have triumphed over challenges such as self-doubt, ill health, addiction, mental illness, cancer diagnoses, caregiving, grief, insecurity, and oppression. You might resonate with some of their struggles and victories. The hardships they faced did not defeat them; instead, they revealed their inner strength.

These stories will inspire and empower you to reach greater heights. If these achievers can rise above the odds and become significant figures in their communities, so can you! If you have been re-created in the image of the Lion of Judah; you too can roar and soar.

BEE Encouraged, My Black Sister!

Dr. Caretha Franks Crawford
Author, Editor and Publisher

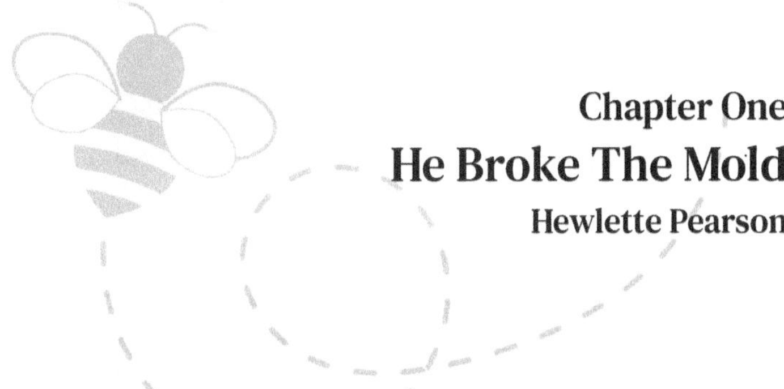

Chapter One
He Broke The Mold
Hewlette Pearson

I had never flown on an airplane before. I was eight years old, and everything felt strange and overwhelming. I watched the airport bustle with people, all moving with purpose, speaking in accents I was not accustomed to. As we boarded the plane, I felt the movement, heard the roaring engines, and suddenly, we were speeding down the runway. Then, as if by magic, we lifted into the sky. The world outside the window seemed surreal—the tiny cars below, the vast blue sky above, and the soft, cotton-like clouds surrounding us. I was in a space I had only seen on television.

Not long into the flight, a food tray was placed before me. It was nothing like the meals I had back home in Jamaica. I poked at it curiously, trying to make sense of the tough meat and the smooth, white mashed potatoes. I distinctly remember struggling to chew the meat, so my father ate it for me. Years later, I learned the meal was steak, mashed potatoes, and string beans. We were flying with Eastern Airlines, heading from Jamaica to Washington, D.C. Though the flight was uneventful, its significance was heavy. My father, brothers, and I were leaving behind everything familiar to start a new life—a life my mother had already begun over four years before us.

Coming to the United States for what some would call "a

better life" did not feel better. I was thrown into an unfamiliar world where everything, from the weather to the culture to the way people spoke. School was the hardest adjustment of all. I sat in class for two and a half months and did no work. I could hear the teacher speaking, see her writing on the blackboard, and watch as she helped other students with their assignments. But none of it made sense to me. I could not understand the language well, and I do not recall her ever coming over to help me personally. Every day, I sat in silence, staring at work I could not complete.

The only times I felt any sense of participation were during gym class and art. I was athletic, I could draw—but academic subjects were beyond my reach. When my teacher spoke to my mother, she explained that while she could technically move me to the next grade, it would serve no purpose. That summer, I was enrolled in summer school, and in the evenings, my mother painstakingly taught me how to read and write. It was an arduous process for both of us—one filled with frustration, tears, and determination. But that's a story for another time.

By the end of summer, we had moved to a different part of the city. This new school experience was different. This period, though academically better, was socially and emotionally devastating. The trauma of being bullied was a wound that would take years to heal.

At first, I didn't understand why I was being targeted. My peers singled me out, and the bullying became relentless. Each year, it grew worse. By fourth grade, my difference had become a spectacle. One day, as I left class for lunch, a group of students performed a song they had rehearsed—about me.

"I believe in wrinkles. She needs an iron to iron her fingers..."

They had taken the melody from the Jackson Sisters' song *I Believe in Miracles* and turned it into a cruel anthem. They laughed and sang while others joined in, pointing, jeering, and poking me. I had nowhere to run, nowhere to hide. I wanted to disappear.

The bullying continued through fifth grade. My teacher, Ms.

Hawkins, eventually took notice of my distress. She allowed me to leave class fifteen minutes early every day so I could get a head start on my walk home—an attempt to escape the mob that followed me, pushing, hitting, and taunting me along the way.

Living in constant fear at school and later encountering subtle forms of rejection and belittlement in adulthood took a toll on my self-worth. I internalized the negativity. The voices of the bullies became the voices in my own mind. I felt inferior, unworthy, and ashamed of my appearance. The way I saw myself was reflected in the colors I wore—dark, muted tones designed to make me invisible.

In college, my choir director confronted me. "Hewlette, you have such a beautiful smile and personality. Why do you wear such dark clothing? Please do not come up in my class again with those colors. Let me see some reds, oranges, light blues..."

At first, it was a struggle. But I complied. And slowly, as I stepped out of my comfort zone, the compliments started coming in. I felt better about myself. But deep inside, I knew I needed a deeper healing—one that wouldn't crumble at the first insult or insecurity that surfaced.

My journey of healing took time, but the turning point came in my early forties. One day, as I was reflecting on God's goodness, I heard His voice gently but firmly say, *"I need you to stop comparing yourself to others."*

I was startled. I hadn't realized how much I had allowed comparison to dictate my view of myself.

"Every time you compare yourself to someone else, you are telling Me I did not do a good job in creating you," He said.

The weight of those words broke me. I wept in sorrow, repentance, and guilt. I cried out to God, asking for forgiveness. At that moment, something in me shifted. The healing I longed for had finally begun. I saw myself through God's eyes. His words silenced the voices that had tormented me for decades. And He gave me a tool to maintain my healing—affirmations.

I began writing affirmations that I would speak over myself daily. Here is one:

- My name is Hewlette Pearson, and no one is like me.
- God loves me, and He is pleased with me.
- I am one of God's most beautiful designs, and everything about me reflects Him.
- I am fearfully and wonderfully made and bring flavor and light wherever I go.
- I am Hewlette Pearson. I love myself, and God is my strength!

For years, I had picked up the broken pieces of my mold, trying to recreate my beauty from what I saw in others. But God showed me that I was His masterpiece—His highest work of art, crafted with excellence. Ephesians 2:10a (New Living Translation) says, *"For we are God's masterpiece..."* That truth transformed me. I began to see myself worthy of love and friendship. My approach to life became one of eagerness and excitement. What a beautiful work of art I am!

The mind is a battlefield, but it is also the gateway to transformation. My greatest enemy was never the trauma of my past—it was my belief in the lies told to me. God taught me to replace those lies with His truth.

If you struggle with comparison, take time to write out the beauty and goodness in you. Speak it over yourself daily. You are one of a kind—God's Masterpiece!

~

Chapter Two

Unmasked: Embracing the Strength Behind the Smile

Dr. Michelle Boone-Thornton

It wasn't until I developed a relationship with God that I truly allowed myself to feel. Growing up, I was always told I was resilient, independent, and capable of navigating my world without much assistance. My parents, perhaps unintentionally, reinforced this perception. My mother's heart problems led to multiple hospitalizations and eventually open-heart surgery. After I was born, my aunt came to live with us to help my mother recover. For the first few years of my life, she was my primary caregiver before returning to her home. That abrupt transition was my first lesson in loss.

I bonded deeply with my older brother, who became my protector and my safe place. But life has a way of reminding you that nothing lasts forever. He passed away as a young adult, and once again, I found myself abandoned by the person I trusted most. Trust became an impossibility. The people I loved and depended on had a way of disappearing. I carried that scar within me, refusing to let anyone in because I knew, eventually, they would leave, too.

On the outside, I looked like I had a great life—happy, successful, and thriving. But I was wearing a mask. I became an expert at pretending everything was fine. I smiled, laughed, and excelled in my pursuits, but inside, I felt empty. I lived my life as an imposter, never allowing anyone to see my true self. This is why I understand the importance of authenticity. I know what it's like to live behind a mask, afraid that if anyone saw the real me, they would walk away.

As a child, I didn't crave attention, but like any child, I wanted to be seen, heard, and engage with my parents. The adults in my life were distracted—my mother was ill, and my father worked two jobs. I learned early on that forming relationships often led to loss, so I chose to protect myself from being hurt again. I was not a child, teen, or even adult who appeared needy; instead, I projected an image of independence and self-sufficiency. But beneath the surface, I longed for companionship and love. After pushing people away for so long, they started to believe I didn't want or need them. In reality, it was a self-sabotaging way to live—wanting to be close but simultaneously keeping people at arm's length. I didn't know any better; I was simply protecting my heart from further hurt and disappointment.

For years, I carried these beliefs into adulthood, living with the expectation that anything good in my life wouldn't last. It wasn't pessimism; it was survival. I braced myself for disappointment as if it were inevitable. I built walls so high that even I couldn't see over them. It wasn't until I encountered God that I began to dismantle them, brick by brick.

My turning point came during a season of utter brokenness. I had spent years striving to be what others expected, ignoring my own identity and needs. Like many Black women, I wore my resilience like armor, shielding myself from pain while silently bearing its weight. But God had a different plan for me. He saw through my facade and whispered, "You are mine. You are seen, and you are loved."

One day, a woman I barely knew spoke a prophecy over me. She told me that God had great plans for my life, that I would speak on international stages and impact countless lives. I smiled politely but dismissed her words as wishful thinking. How could someone who felt so unseen and unworthy achieve such greatness? Yet, this wasn't the first time someone had spoken life over me. Years earlier, a pastor had shared a similar vision. I ignored it then too.

It wasn't until years later that I realized God had been orchestrating a symphony of hope all along. I began to lean into His promises, trusting that His plan for my life was far greater than the narrative I had written for myself. Psalm 139:14 says, "I praise you because I am fearfully and wonderfully made; your works are wonderful, I know that full well." For the first time, I began to believe it.

That experience changed me. It taught me that resilience isn't about enduring hardship alone; it's about allowing God to carry the weight we were never meant to bear. I began to see myself as God sees me—not as an invisible afterthought but as a beloved child with unique gifts and a divine purpose.

I had spent much of my life content with trusting only in myself, believing that self-reliance was the only way to survive. But that belief left me feeling empty. God created us to help and support each other. Human connection is important; we need one another. It was only when I allowed myself to lean on God and the people He placed in my life that I found true fulfillment.

Today, I live with a renewed sense of hope and determination. I've embraced the truth that my value isn't tied to what I can do for others or how well I meet their expectations. My worth comes from the One who created me. As Jeremiah 29:11 reminds us, "For I know the plans I have for you," declares the Lord, "plans to prosper you and not to harm you, plans to give you hope and a future."

To my sisters reading this, know that God sees you. He sees your struggles, your sacrifices, and your silent tears. You are not invisible to Him. Your steps are ordered, even when the path seems unclear. Don't let the enemy's lies convince you that you're unworthy of joy and peace. You are fearfully and wonderfully made, equipped with gifts and potential waiting to be unlocked by God's touch.

If you take nothing else from my story, let it be this: resilience isn't about being strong all the time. It's about surrendering your burdens to God and trusting Him to work all things together for your good (Romans 8:28). You are not alone, and you don't have to face life's challenges in isolation. God has placed people in your life to walk alongside you, just as He placed others in mine.

Your story isn't over. The best is yet to come. Trust in God's promises, and you will see His goodness unfold in ways you never imagined. You are seen, you are loved, and you are destined for greatness.

~

"It taught me that resilience isn't about enduring hardship alone; it's about allowing God to carry the weight we were never meant to bear."

Chapter Three
When Love Calls
You to Battle:
A Caregiver's Journey of Faith and
Resilience - Theresa Royal Brown

aregiving is not for the faint of heart. It is a calling, a test of endurance, and in my case, an unrelenting battle between life and loss. When my husband, Charles, fell ill in early 2022, I had no idea the depth of resilience, faith, and strength that it would require of me. But God knew. And He was with me every step of the way.

The Beginning of the Battle

It all started when my husband, Charles, took his third COVID shot in December 2021. By the end of January 2022, he was sick—really sick. I rushed him to the hospital, where he was diagnosed with COVID. He recovered, but something wasn't right. He wasn't the same man. His energy was low, his weight was dropping, and his body was struggling in ways we couldn't quite understand.

Then, in March 2022, the unthinkable happened. We lost our home. A fraudulent investor had manipulated the system and stolen the title to our house. We had fought in court for years, but the stress of the battle had drained us both. When we lost, it took a piece of Charles with it. The weight of it all bore down on him.

By June, his body was failing. Breathing became difficult. Walking long distances felt impossible. We thought it would pass, but it didn't. In July, I could no longer ignore the severity of his condition. I rushed him to the hospital, and this would mark the first of twelve hospital stays over the next two years—each one more grueling than the last.

Fighting for His Life

That first hospital stay lasted 10 days. I sat by Charles' bedside for 12 to 14 hours each day, watching, praying, pleading with God. He was weak—so weak that his spirit felt tired. Doctors discovered he had a perforated intestine. Their recommendation? Exploratory surgery. But something in my spirit told me no. I had to fight for him.

Instead of surgery, I insisted on a liquid diet and strong antibiotics, believing in my heart that his body could heal with the proper support. But for four agonizing days, I watched as death hovered over him. And then, in a moment I will never forget, he looked at me and said, "Maybe it would be best for you if I just wasn't here."

My heart shattered.

But something inside me—something fierce and unbreakable—rose. I refused to let him give up. I knew I needed help. Charles had always been a private man, but this battle required an army. So, I called on my faith-family.

I rallied 20 pastors, prophets, and prayer warriors from across the country. I put the phone on speaker in his hospital room and let them do what they did best—pray. And oh, did they pray! The power in that room was undeniable.

As the prayers went forth, I saw something shift in Charles. His eyes regained their light. His spirit came back into focus. And by day six, he was up and moving. By day nine, his intestine had healed itself. And on day ten, he was released.

It was a miracle. But it was just the beginning.

The Unseen Toll of Caregiving

Between 2022 and 2024, Charles was hospitalized twelve times. Each stay was its own battle, its own heartbreak, its own test of endurance. And through every one of them, I was there. Sitting. Watching. Advocating. Praying.

Caregiving is a relentless, exhausting, and often thankless job. For family caregivers like me, it is unpaid and unrecognized. It is waking up in the middle of the night to check on your loved one's breathing. It is lifting, turning, and repositioning their body, even when the caregiver's back is screaming in pain. It is fighting for their dignity when doctors and nurses treat them like just another case.

I know this struggle well. I had done it before—with my father. I was his caregiver for eight years before he passed in 2018. One day, he fell outside, and in an effort to lift his fluid-filled, 185-pound body, I heard something snap in my back. To this day, I still live with pain.

Caregiving doesn't just leave scars on the heart; it leaves them on the body, too.

But for all the hardship, there is love. There is the joy of seeing them smile, the warmth of knowing they are still here, the sacred privilege of being their lifeline. I wouldn't trade that for anything.

Lessons in Resilience and Self-Care

If I've learned anything, it's that caregiving requires more than strength. It requires strategy. It requires boundaries. It requires self-care because you cannot pour from an empty cup.

I learned to:

- Prioritize my health—because if I break down, who will be there for Charles?
- Ask for help—even when it feels uncomfortable.
- Take breaks—because even five minutes of fresh air can be healing.
- Stay connected—to God, to my friends, to my support system.
- Celebrate the small victories—because in caregiving, every little win matters.

A Final Word of Encouragement

If you are a caregiver, I see you. I know the weight of your exhaustion, the ache of your sacrifices, the silent tears you cry when no one is watching. I see the frustration, the fear, the moments where you feel like you are drowning. But I also know this—God sees you, too.

You are not alone. You are stronger than you think. And the love you are pouring into your loved one? It matters. God sees it, and others feel it.

Caregiving is not just about helping someone live—it is about showing them they are not alone in the fight. And my dear sister, neither are you.

Hold on. Keep going. And when you feel like you can't take another step, remember: God's strength is made perfect in your weakness.

You are resilient. You are powerful. And most of all, you are not forgotten.

Chapter Four
Shattered Links
Judy Ann Reid

For 29 years, I waited—patiently, prayerfully, hopefully. I believed that if I chose wisely, loved deeply, and trusted in God's timing, God would bless me with a husband who cherished me. I had seen enough broken marriages to know I didn't want anything half-hearted or temporary. So when I finally said, "I do," I did so with the full belief that I had found my forever—a man of faith, of integrity, of love.

At least, that's who he appeared to be.

He was charming, articulate, and attentive. He spoke the language of faith fluently, attended church regularly, and showed interest in the things that mattered to me. To the outside world, he looked like a God-fearing gentleman—exactly the kind of man worth waiting nearly three decades to marry.

But that image didn't last long.

Soon after the wedding, the mask began to slip. My husband's gentle tone turned sharp. His attentiveness morphed into surveillance. My routines, my phone calls, even my silences were under scrutiny. When he questioned me, it wasn't with love. The questions were suspicious and demanding. Slowly, I realized I hadn't married a partner. I had married a controller.

He interfered in my professional life without my consent—

contacting colleagues, sowing doubt, and undermining my credibility. These weren't naive mistakes. They were calculated acts of manipulation. When I confronted him, he didn't deny it. Instead, he twisted scripture to justify his behavior, quoting our then-pastor and weaponizing the Word of God.

The Bible, once my source of comfort, became his tool of control.

He used verses like "a man shall leave his father and mother and cleave to his wife" not to create unity, but to isolate me from my support system. He portrayed closeness with my family as disobedience to God. And for a time, I believed him. I wanted to honor my husband and my faith. But deep down, I knew his actions weren't godly, nor were they love.

He sent money to my friends through CashApp, thanking them for "bringing me into his life." What seemed like a generous gesture was actually manipulation. He obtained their contact information without my consent and used it to exert influence and present himself as thoughtful and spiritual. But those who knew better saw through it.

During holidays, he kept me from speaking to his guests—cutting me out of conversations, controlling every interaction. Even his friends noticed. The warm, welcoming man they saw in public didn't exist behind closed doors. That man—my husband—was no man of faith. He was a master manipulator hiding behind religion.

He used the image of godliness to feed his need for control.

And I'll never forget this truth: I married a god man—but not a good man.

On paper, he looked perfect. His smile, his church attendance, his charm—they painted a beautiful picture. But they were just brushstrokes covering a dark reality. My husband wasn't committed to our marriage. He was committed to his image. His words in public were sweet, but private, they cut like knives.

It was never about love. It was about power.

Leaving wasn't easy. How do you walk away from what you waited so long for? But there came a moment when I realized that loving God, loving truth, and loving myself had to come before clinging to a fantasy. So, I left. Not because I gave up on love, but because I finally understood what love is not.

Have you ever wanted to scream, but no sound came out? That was me. I kept telling myself it would get better—but it didn't. The pain of betrayal and spiritual manipulation cut deep. The ones I trusted most stood in alliance against me. Friends, I considered family supported him, even after seeing how he treated me.

But that's when I turned to the One who never left me: God.

I began to pray—not just formally, but as if I were talking to my best friend. I opened my Bible, clung to scriptures that spoke to my heart, and found strength in verses like Deuteronomy 31:6 (NLT):

"So be strong and courageous! Do not be afraid and do not panic before them. For the Lord your God will personally go ahead of you. He will neither fail you nor abandon you."

I worshipped in my quiet time. I encouraged myself daily. I reminded myself of every time God had carried me before—and I believed He would carry me again. And He did. I didn't heal by my own strength; I healed through the power of God. He lifted the pain, piece by piece. I'm living proof that He will never leave or forsake us.

I cut ties with the pastor who enabled the abuse. I walked away from the church that dressed manipulation as ministry. I reclaimed my voice, my peace, and my purpose.

My family never stopped loving me. My real friends stayed close. Some protected me even when I couldn't see the danger. I lost people, too—friends whose envy turned them into allies of the man who mistreated me. But I gained clarity.

This marriage taught me exactly what love is not.

Love isn't control. It isn't manipulation. It isn't spiritual domination. Love doesn't isolate, shame, or diminish. Love builds, heals, and protects. It never requires you to lose your God-given identity just to be accepted.

I no longer carry shame for the love I gave. I was sincere. My only mistake was trusting someone who hid their true self until it was too late. But it wasn't a waste. Every scar taught me something about my worth, my strength, and my discernment.

I share my story not as a victim, but as a survivor.

Psychological abuse happens more than we talk about—especially in faith communities where silence is mistaken for submission, contentment, and often holiness. In faith communities, we are told to pray more, submit more, and endure more. But prayer won't change someone who refuses to change. Submission isn't the same as surrendering your soul.

The man I married wasn't my forever. He was my lesson.

I no longer believe that staying silent is a sign of righteousness.

And now, with strength, clarity, and peace, I move forward. I still believe in God. I still believe in love.

If you've been silenced by someone who used love or scripture to control you, I see you.

- You are not wrong for leaving.
- You are not unlovable.
- You are not broken.
- You are being rebuilt.
- And your forever begins with you.

~

Chapter Five

Overcoming Oppression: A Journey of Forgiveness, Healing, and Leadership

Beverly Claiborne

Overcoming oppression is not an easy path; it requires courage, unwavering support, and a commitment to your own well-being. But as difficult as it may be, you are not alone. There are people, resources, and faith that can guide you through this challenging experience. For me, it was through God's love and guidance that I found my healing, and it is in His strength that I continue to stand strong.

When dealing with oppression or verbal abuse from a person of great stature or a loved one, this behavior can make you feel unworthy. Especially when we depend on the individual for spiritual guidance and leadership. I've experienced this several times and it put me in a state of mind that began to stiffer my growth and doubt myself. But as I prayed and sought clarity, the Holy Spirit spoke to me, teaching me about *the power of forgiveness.* He reminded me that everyone is dealing with something; we all carry burdens. However, that does not justify the hurtful behavior of others. No one has the right to belittle or verbally abuse another.

When we choose to forgive, we are doing it for ourselves, not the person who hurt us. Forgiveness sets us free from resentment and pain. Verbal abuse made me question my worth, but through prayer, I heard from God. He spoke directly to me, reminding me that there are people and places in this world that are an abomination to Him.

True leadership reflects values that align with God's teachings —integrity, love, and service. But what happens when those in leadership positions fail to embody those principles? What happens when leadership falls short?

This is where I found myself—struggling with the reality of leaders in authority behaving badly. The more I reflected, the more I realized that God's word remains true: "By their fruit, you will know them." A good tree cannot bear bad fruit, and a bad tree cannot bear good fruit. The action of any leader reflects their heart at that very moment. I had to choose if I'd allow these actions to define my sense of self-worth. Through my struggle, I found peace in God's word. I put my trust in Him, knowing that when leaders fail to lead with integrity and love, they fail those they serve!

Through my struggle, I found peace in God's word and put my trust in Him. I realized that when leaders fail to lead with integrity and love, they fail those they are meant to serve. Had I not been guided by the Holy Spirit to forgive; I would have been left questioning my worth. We must cling to God's promises, understanding that we all fall short and must rely on His promises for our lives. If we let our emotions or the behavior of toxic leaders control us, our lives will be tainted by their negativity. As Christians, we are called to let the fruit of God's Spirit be evident in our lives, leaving behind a legacy that transforms others.

The Bible speaks clearly about the power of resilience. We are told to put on the full armor of God and stand firm against the schemes of the devil. His word encourages us to be strong and courageous, trusting that He is with us through every trial.

As I leaned on God's word, I found the strength to forgive— not because the other person deserved it, but because I needed it. Forgiveness became my pathway to freedom. It unlocked the chains that kept me bound in bitterness. With forgiveness came healing, not just for my relationship with the person who hurt me, but for my own heart and soul.

The Holy Spirit, our Comforter, walked with me every step of the way. In moments of turmoil, He revealed the truth to me. Through His wisdom, I understood that forgiveness is not just about absolving others; it's about liberating ourselves. It's about letting go of emotional and spiritual baggage that weighs us down. Through His guidance, I found clarity, peace, and strength.

Here are five ways to jumpstart your healing journey:

1. Recognize and Acknowledge the Oppression

Overcoming oppression is painful, but it also offers an opportunity for growth and a deeper understanding of leadership. Leadership is not about titles, it's about service, integrity, and love. A good leader leads with empathy, kindness, and respect, creating an environment where others can thrive. If a leader fails in this area, it becomes an opportunity to understand that leadership is not about power but about the ability to help others grow and flourish.

2. Seek Support. Seeking support from loved ones. Seek healing through prayer and reflection. Trust in God's word and know that He will guide you every step of the way. And when the time comes, forgive—not for the other person, but for your own healing. It is essential to surround yourself with a strong support system, people who lift you up and remind you that healing is possible. The journey may be long, but you do not have to walk it alone.

3. Set Clear Boundaries

One of the most powerful lessons I learned is the importance of boundaries. Setting boundaries protects your emotional well-being and fosters respect in your relationships. It's about teaching others how to treat you and taking care of yourself. We must create boundaries in our relationships to protect our inner peace. Boundaries prevent emotional burnout and ensure that we protect ourselves from further harm. They allow us to engage with others from a place of strength and self-respect. We can't forget that respecting the boundaries of others is just as important as setting up our own.

4. See a Licensed Counselor or Join Reputable Support Groups

When verbal abuse feels overwhelming, professional help can make a world of difference. Licensed counselors and support groups offer a safe space for you to express your feelings and receive guidance from trained professionals. These support networks can help you process your emotions, find clarity, and take the necessary steps toward healing.

5. Document the Oppression

Sometimes, verbal abuse can be hard to put into words, but documenting the experience is crucial for your healing and future accountability. Keep a record of specific instances—dates, times, and the exact words spoken. This documentation is not about holding onto resentment but about giving yourself clarity. It's about taking control of your narrative, recognizing the truth, and preparing yourself for necessary steps, whether that's seeking help, confronting the person, or making decisions about your future. Journaling can help you process the hurt and reclaim your voice.

As Christians, we are called to be salt and light in the world. Whether at home, in the workplace, our places of worship, or in the community, let us strive to embody the qualities of true leadership—serving with love, leading with integrity, and always honoring God above all else. We are called to lead with compassion and strength, and through our resilience, we will rise above any obstacle. By holding ourselves to the standard of love, truth, and integrity, we can overcome any challenge and live out our purpose.

~

Chapter Six
One Night, One Choice
Lakia Bradley

I t began as a night like any other, the kind of evening shift I had worked countless times before. I usually parked in the garage across from the hotel, but for reasons I still cannot explain, I chose to park downstairs. That one small decision—one choice—became the first thread in a series of moments that would alter the course of my life.

After parking and clocking in, I headed upstairs to begin my shift. The night started with a seemingly harmless inconvenience: a guest who needed help parking because she had forgotten her wallet. I assisted her without much thought. Shortly after, several late arrivals checked in, all preparing for a large conference at the nearby convention center. None of this was unusual. Busy nights came with the job.

But everything changed in a matter of minutes.

I had just finished checking in a guest when I noticed a man stumbling near the guest's vehicle. I assumed they were together, especially when the guest walked back inside with him and pointed him toward the front desk. As he approached, I could tell immediately that he was intoxicated—his steps heavy, his speech sluggish. This was not new to me. As a night auditor, I had encountered intoxicated guests many times. I remained calm and followed protocol.

The assailant insisted he had a room, so I asked for his identification and checked the system. Nothing came up. Then he claimed the reservation was under someone else's name, yet that name was not in our system either. I suggested he call his friend. He pretended to dial a number, pressing random buttons on his phone. I still believed this was just another person in need of assistance.

But in one instant, everything shifted.

He looked at me, balled up his fist, and said, "Watch this." Before I could register what he meant, he swung and punched me directly in the eye. Pain exploded through my face. Shock flooded my body. My mind scrambled to comprehend what had just happened.

Instinct took over.

I immediately called 911 while he ran toward the elevator, attempting to escape. When he realized he couldn't flee, he turned back toward me—this time as an aggressor determined to inflict more harm. He chased me around the front desk, yelling, throwing a large plant, and lunging at me.

But God protected me. In the middle of chaos, He made a way.

I ran out the front door and alerted the guest I had just checked in moments earlier. "Please call 911—I've been attacked!" The guest rushed inside with me, ready to defend me, and together we dodged objects the assailant hurled from the front desk area. Eventually, the man ran down the hallway and managed to get out of sight.

He might have escaped—but God had other plans.

The same guest I had checked in tracked him from a safe distance and guided police officers to him. Minutes later, they apprehended him. When my manager arrived, I was finally able to go home to my children—shaken, bruised, but alive.

The physical damage to my face was minimal compared to what could have happened. But the internal wounds were far deeper. Old battles with anxiety resurfaced, gripping my thoughts and stealing my peace. I found myself replaying the moment over and over—the fist, the chase, the fear. The "what ifs" haunted me.

Yet even in my darkest mental moments, God provided.

He sent me a therapist who helped me untangle the trauma. He surrounded me with support. But one Sunday morning, everything felt overwhelmingly heavy. I wasn't working. The memories were relentless. My finances had been reduced to nearly nothing— I had received only one week of pay after the incident—and I was struggling to take care of my three children.

That morning, I felt defeated. But God was not finished.

As I prayed, cried, and searched Scripture for comfort, He gave me an idea—one that would turn my pain into purpose. He placed in my heart the vision for a seminar for teenagers titled:

"One Night, One Choice: How Alcohol and Drugs Can Change Everything."

This seminar is designed to explore how substances impair human functionality, decision-making, and behavior—how one moment of intoxication can alter not only your life, but someone else's. It would also illuminate the spiritual reality behind our choices and remind young people that God calls them to wisdom, self-control, and accountability.

That day, I made a vow:

"From Brokenness to Boldness — A Voice God Restored."

This Teen Awareness Initiative is developed to empower young people to make safer choices, look out for one another, and speak truth when it matters most. I wanted to help them understand what I learned firsthand: that one person's reckless decision can change someone else's life forever.

Although I still battle the memories of that night, I refuse to let it silence me or steal who I am. I am still the kind, gentle soul who helps others in crisis. In fact, this experience reignited a voice I had forgotten—the voice that once guided others through their hardships using wisdom, compassion, and God's truth.

To anyone who has survived an assault, let me speak directly to your heart:

This happened "to" you, not "because" of you.

You are not to blame for someone else's sin, violence, or loss of control. Do not allow fear or shame to keep you from the full, abundant life God designed for you. Your story does not end in trauma. It may very well begin there, but it can grow into strength, courage, and purpose.

Let your experience give you a voice—a strong one that speaks out against acts of cruelty and injustice so that others might pause before destroying another person's life with one reckless decision. You are not a victim stuck in the moment of your pain. You are a survivor with a testimony that can bring awareness, healing, and change.

One night changed my life. One choice nearly ended my peace. But another choice—God's choice to use my pain for purpose— changed everything again.

And now, I choose to walk boldly in the calling placed before me:

To speak. To empower. To teach. To rise.

One night. One choice. One voice—mine—refusing to stay silent.

～

Chapter Seven
My Mental Health
Journey To Wholeness
Tonya Sinclair Swindell

Journey is defined as "an act of traveling from one place to another." That's exactly what it's been like for me to experience mental health challenges starting at 18 years old until now at 51. Thankfully, my journey has been one of peace despite the emotional ups and downs that I have faced along the way.

My mental health journey began in February 1992 during my freshman year of college at UNC Wilmington (UNCW). It was a very quaint and inviting liberal arts school in Eastern North Carolina, and I loved it there! Students were very friendly, and I liked the relaxed, casual atmosphere.

Ever since my junior year in high school, I had a boyfriend named Regan. While I was at UNCW, he was in Virginia Beach, VA, serving as a submariner for the US Navy. One weekend, he visited and asked me to marry him while we were sitting in his parked car next to my school's baseball diamond. I said, "Yes," after which he placed a beautiful solitaire on my left ring finger. Shortly after that, he returned to his duty station.

While I was miles away from my fiancé, I kept a very disciplined schedule that mostly involved eating in the cafeteria, attending classes, and completing homework. I also spent up to an hour each day praying and reading my Bible. On Sundays, I attended church with a friend. Those activities were very important to me, especially since I gave my life to Christ in September 1989.

I sang alto in my school's gospel choir. And I enjoyed traveling to different churches to share my talent. I also joined the Baptist Student Union, which was a good way to socialize while learning about God.

I wasn't sleeping very well, but it wasn't because of my quiet yet outgoing roommate named Tracy. She wasn't around very much because she was out hanging with friends. One time, she noticed an ample amount of tears trickling down my face. I honestly couldn't explain why I was crying. In hindsight, I believe that was one of the first signs that my mental health needed attention.

On another day, my eyes popped open as I lay in bed asleep. When I awakened, it felt like a ball of energy was rushing through my body. So I decided to go running. It was around 2 a.m., and my wardrobe, including a hair bonnet, pajama top and bottoms, and a pair of bedroom slippers, didn't even deter me.

I ran until I felt tired. Then I walked to the campus police station and asked to be driven to my dormitory. Looking back, that was another red flag indicating intervention was needed.

I began skipping class to "preach" on campus, mostly reading Bible verses out loud on a street corner, hoping students would feel convicted by the words I spoke. I gradually isolated myself, eating meals alone in my room instead of in the cafeteria. I was cordial to my schoolmates, but when it came to having fun, I didn't enjoy many activities.

I tried to engage girls in my hall by slowly walking into their rooms. Then I would ask, "May I talk to you about Jesus?" I might have been more successful at that if it hadn't been 3 a.m., when the girls were trying to sleep.

I used the payphone to call my mom weekly. I looked forward to hearing her voice and updating her on my activities. Despite significant changes in my life, I got good grades, which pleased my parents.

My mom was a great listener. All of her years as a wonderful mother to me and my older brother, and her professional work as a social worker, helped her realize that something was wrong with her "baby." My father's experience as a Missionary Baptist pastor and a high school vice principal made him very attentive and concerned about my behavior.

Mama came to visit me. And while there, one of my requests was for her to drive me to Pizza Hut to get breadsticks. I had been fasting a lot; therefore, my body craved bread to break the fast.

While riding in the car, I had conflicting thoughts. One was to ball up my fist and punch Mama in the face. The other was to open my passenger's side door and jump out. Thankfully, those thoughts never turned into actions.

While I became increasingly anxious, Mama continued to drive nervously. The whole time she was talking to God out loud, asking Him for mercy and guidance. It was dark outside, and once we returned to campus, I took off running. At one point, I stepped onto the hood and eventually the top of someone's car. A very polite female student tried to convince me to come down.

That night, I fearlessly navigated around barking dogs, jumped over fences, and rang doorbells to ask homeowners if I could talk to them about Jesus. Eventually, I got tired, and by that time, Mama and a campus policeman stood in the street waiting for me. I walked calmly to the police car, got in, and rode back to my dorm.

While using the communal bathroom, I heard someone open the door and then quickly close it without entering. I imagined it was a fellow student who feared interacting with me because of my behavior. Soon after that, I realized I needed help, as I began to appreciate the seriousness of my situation.

The next day, Mama drove to New Bern, NC, my hometown, and I was admitted to Crossroads, an inpatient psychiatric unit. I stayed there for 18 days and was prescribed lithium, a mood stabilizer, for the diagnosis of bipolar disorder. While hospitalized, I attended occupational therapy groups in which we discussed stress management, anger management, and how to be assertive. We also did craft activities, like painting and woodworking.

After being hospitalized, I met with a licensed clinical social worker on an outpatient basis. Although I eventually broke up with Regan, he helped to heal my heart by writing encouraging letters. We eventually got back together and married in December 1992.

In August 1993, my psychiatrist took me off of lithium, which was an answer to prayer since a different doctor told me that I'd be on it for the rest of my life. Two years later, I enrolled in the occupational therapy (OT) program at the Medical University of South Carolina. I graduated with a bachelor's degree in OT in May 1997, and I have been working within my profession for almost 28 years. In 2007, I also completed my Master's Degree in Community Health Education and Health Promotion at Old Dominion University.

Since becoming older, I've had occasional episodes for which I needed medication and talk therapy. Both of them are still valuable tools. Despite ups and downs, I'm hopeful that my shared experiences will be motivating to individuals on their mental health journey to wholeness.

Chapter Eight
Cancer Chose
the Wrong Girl!
Dr. Caretha Franks Crawford

The word "cancer" evokes many thoughts and scenarios, most of which are negative. It's a dreadful disease that does not discriminate and is responsible for countless casualties. Unfortunately, many families know the devastating impact of this disease all too well, and mine is no exception. I believed I had managed to evade cancer's grasp until December 7, 2022, when my doctor's words hit me like a bolt of lightning: was he really saying what I thought I heard—cancer in my breast? My mind raced through a whirlwind of emotions, as if I were in a time warp. I envisioned treatments that would lead to the loss of body parts, including my hair, and downtime from activities I love, like traveling. I was also haunted by memories of loved ones who lost their battle with this disease. For a moment, time seemed to stand still.

My experience in unsolicited competition would prove beneficial now. I quickly realized the need to adopt a strong stance and an unpredictable offensive strategy, principles I learned from my boxing training.

After a fun day of making greeting cards with my mentee, Lakia, I was relaxing in my La-Z-Boy chair when I reached across my body with my left arm and brushed against my left breast. The touch felt unexpectedly tender and sore, causing me to scream, "Ouch!" I was baffled by what had just happened.

When I removed my pajama top, I discovered that my left breast was sensitive and swollen. My primary care doctor was equally confused when I visited her the following day. She realized that my case was beyond her expertise and promptly sought the advice of a breast care specialist. Although she couldn't reach him immediately, she prioritized contacting him for the next day.

At 8:30 a.m., my phone rang. My doctor gave me the specialist's phone number and instructions on how to proceed.

After about a 10-day wait, I was finally able to see the specialist, who was a Vietnamese-born physician. In his gentle manner, he guided me through his prognosis, reassuring me that, more than likely, what I was experiencing was not cancer but rather papilloma, which is a benign tumor. He explained that cancer typically does not cause pain until the later stages. He performed a needle biopsy and gave me a prescription for a sonogram of my left breast, explaining that if it showed papilloma, his recommendation would be to remove it.

On the day of my scheduled sonogram, the technician informed me that my insurance required me to have a mammogram instead. I explained that my doctor had explicitly ordered a sonogram, not a mammogram. Additionally, I had undergone a mammogram three months prior, which showed no concerns. Sitting in the waiting area, I felt cold, hungry, and frustrated as I waited for authorization.

The mammogram was the final decision. It was excruciating, especially since my breast was already tender. A few minutes after the mammogram, the technician delivered the news I had been waiting for: nothing suspicious was detected, and I was free to go.

Good news always makes your heart leap for joy, even if it's short-lived. A few months later, while alone in North Carolina, I felt moisture on my gown. My left breast was discharging, which caused me concern. The following day, I contacted my doctor, who emphatically told me to get a sonogram, not a mammogram, stating that he couldn't see what he needed on a mammogram. However, when I called to schedule the sonogram, the scheduler insisted that I needed a mammogram first. At that moment, the determined Southern girl inside me stood up. I reiterated my doctor's orders to the scheduler, but she was unyielding. Clearly, I needed someone with more authority to handle the situation. I called my doctor's office and explained what was happening. The office manager assured me that she would take care of it from there. She called back to say that someone in a higher position would contact me. The next day, a woman from the imaging office called and apologized for the scheduler's behavior. My sonogram was then scheduled for the following week.

The sonogram went smoothly and confirmed what the doctor suspected: papilloma. He recommended a biopsy to determine the next steps, which ultimately led to the decision to remove the papilloma. Surgery was scheduled for December 5, 2022. This wasn't my first experience with the removal of a benign tumor; I had also had a tumor removed from my left breast when I was 26. The day of the surgery was a little unnerving. I worried about not waking up from the anesthesia. My doctor and husband later told me that I remained under anesthesia longer than expected. As I was coming around, I heard the gentle voice of the Lord say, "I have more work for you to do; follow my voice."

Lean in, ladies; this might save your life or the life of a loved one.

What I didn't know at the time was that my surgeon performed two surgeries in one that day. When he called me two days after the surgery, I thought it was merely a courtesy call to see how I was doing post-surgery. This was true, but he had more news to share. My surgeon explained that the surgery went well, but after he finished and prepared me for discharge, he felt compelled to take another look at the area. Upon examination, he noticed something concerning, so he reopened the site and removed the tissue in question. When the lab examined this tissue, it revealed the presence of cancer.

Consider this for a moment: the original intent of the surgery was to remove papilloma. Everything appeared to go smoothly—papilloma removed, I was stitched up, and ready to go—with cancer still in my breast. It was only through divine intervention that the surgeon decided to check again, using a new machine at the hospital. The tumor had been hidden beneath cartilage and had gone undetected by a mammogram, sonogram, MRI, and biopsy.

Proverbs 16:9 (NKJV) states, "A man's heart plans his way, but the Lord directs his steps." Without this intervention during my surgery, who knows how long the cancer could have remained undetected and possibly spread further? Fortunately, the tumor was tiny, and the prognosis was very good. My recommendation was to undergo a second surgery (technically, a third) to ensure that all the cancer was removed and to complete four weeks of radiation treatment. I rang the bell at the Bowie Cancer Center after finishing my radiation on Good Friday, April 7, 2023. Only God could have orchestrated that date!

My experience with breast cancer treatment was not as painful or devastating as that of many other women, including my sister, Carol, who passed away from triple-negative breast cancer in 1999. However, God knows how to encourage and reward us when we submit to Him. Six days after completing my radiation treatments, on April 13, 2023, I stood alongside other esteemed preachers as we were inducted into the Martin Luther King Jr. Board of Preachers at Morehouse College in Atlanta, Georgia. My heart was full of gratitude. Following the induction ceremony, my plus-one, Pastor Lea Philippe, and I drove to Montgomery, Alabama, to view the commemorative brick paver outside the Rosa Parks Museum with my name inscribed on it. These recognitions felt like a clear message from God: "I see you." Despite the real struggles, I know that God is fighting for me!

Sisters, God sees you too. However, we have a role to play in our health journey. Follow the medical community's recommended guidelines for breast health. Be your own advocate. Don't settle for what professionals tell you if you feel something is wrong. Speak up, stand firm, and advocate for your own well-being. During my first visit with my oncologist/radiologist—whom I truly appreciate—we discussed how my future mammograms should be scheduled. In the end, she acknowledged that I was right to insist on what I felt was best for me.

Cancer may have thought it found a hiding place in my breast, but God had other plans!

As a result of my diagnosis, I wrote an encouragement booklet for those battling this disease, titled "POWER for the Journey: Inspiration and Empowerment for Your Breast Cancer Journey." I am also producing a film to educate, empower, and minister to not only those on this journey but, also to all Black women and their loved ones.

Didn't I tell you, cancer chose the wrong girl!

~

"Without this intervention during my surgery, who knows how long the cancer could have remained undetected and possibly spread further?"

Chapter Nine

God Changed My Life, While Saving My Life: My Testimony

Carolyn P. C. Simms

I didn't have time for another major heart attack—certainly not me, the busy advocate! I have places to go and people to encourage.

Everything was going as expected, and I felt great on the morning of July 24, 2024. Unbeknownst to me, however, a disruptor was lurking, planning to challenge my wonderful life. The morning progressed as usual: I ate breakfast and went about my daily routine before leaving home for Bible study. This Bible study would be a bit different because a young guest minister was scheduled to give his trial sermon in hopes of becoming the next minister of the church. The church had organized a celebration to support and encourage him, raising funds to buy him proper clothing and gifting him a tie.

After Bible study, I decided to donate blood at a local blood drive. My friend from church suggested we go to lunch instead, but I preferred to help others rather than spend time together over a meal. So, I donated blood and ran some errands.

After my busy yet satisfying start to the day, I returned home. However, while getting out of my car, I fainted and fell in my driveway. The fall left me paralyzed from my neck to my feet. It was the quick action of my next-door neighbors, who witnessed the incident, that God used to save my life. They helped me into my home and asked if they could call 911, but I hesitated. I was praying for God to save me so that I could continue to serve Him by serving others.

I was dehydrated, and the ninety-degree humidity caused me to suffer a heat stroke. The fall also resulted in a head and back injury. My attempts to reach family members for help were unsuccessful. My sister lived far away, my brother was too busy, and my nephew, who is a nurse, didn't answer his phone. However, on his way home, my nephew decided to stop by my house without knowing that I had tried to call him. When he walked in, I was exhibiting all the symptoms of a heart attack, including extreme chest pain.

Realizing what was happening, my nephew gave me aspirin to slow the progression of the symptoms until the ambulance arrived. I managed to walk to the ambulance and get onto the stretcher. My brother, Mike, who had been too busy earlier, came and broke down in tears when he realized the gravity of the situation. My nephew was also in tears. I felt reassured that God was watching over me; who else could have orchestrated such a scenario? Confident in God and His healing power, I told my family, "Just lock my door; I'll be back home."

As usual, I talked all the way to the hospital, while the young, inexperienced paramedic struggled to connect the IV. He tried three times and failed each time. Despite being in pain, after the third attempt, I asked him to please stop. After all, the hospital was just minutes away. Upon arrival, I was whisked directly into surgery. The medical personnel sprang into action, cutting off my dress and bra, and proceeded with the surgery without anesthesia due to my head injury. I was awake during the four to five-hour procedure. I entered surgery at 3:00 PM and was transferred to the ICU at 8:00 PM. As you can imagine, I was hungry and still in pain.

My dear sister, Audrey, stayed with me in the ICU the first night. She asked the staff for a sedative to help keep me quiet because I couldn't help but praise God and give Him glory for saving my life. He answered my prayers, and I was making plans to continue serving God by serving others.

I returned home on July 27th after a three-day hospital stay. My sisters and daughter, Evelyn, took turns caring for me until I regained my strength. I began intensive heart rehabilitation in September and continued until December 2024. My therapy sessions were three times a week, in addition to participating in nutrition classes.

I celebrated my 75th birthday as a heart attack survivor, surrounded by my entire family. God is so good and faithful; He kept me here for a reason.

I fulfilled my promise to God. In the new year, I completed Caregiver Ambassador training to help encourage caregivers to prioritize their own well-being as well as that of others.

God alone brought me through the challenges of 2024. I now live with 50% of my heart function remaining. By God's grace, I was able to sing a solo, "The Impossible Dream," at my high school class reunion 75th birthday party. I remain actively involved in my local church, Sharpe Road Church of Christ. In April 2025, I gave a speech on self-care to widows, encouraging them to prioritize their own well-being and not neglect their medical care and personal needs.

You have read my testimony of God's grace and faithfulness. Who wouldn't serve my omnipotent God? All glory belongs to Him!

~

Chapter Ten
Grief, Faith and Healing
Rhonda Murphy Lindo

Grief is an unwelcome companion. It enters our lives suddenly and unapologetically, often leaving us shattered and questioning everything—including our faith. If you've ever lost someone you deeply loved, you know that grief isn't something you don't "get over" —it's something you learn to live with, and eventually, something you grow through.

I lost my father on August 19, 2021, in a car accident that wasn't his fault. One moment, he was here—visiting me unexpectedly, calling me "little girl" like he always did, laughing about Harold's lawn—and the next, he was gone. I couldn't believe it. I didn't want to believe it. My heart was broken in ways I didn't know were possible. The man who had survived two serious illnesses and the COVID-19 pandemic—who had spent his life checking in on others—was suddenly gone, just like that.

I questioned God. I prayed for answers. I tried grief counseling. I searched for peace, but the pain was unrelenting. Why would God allow this? Why now, when my father was finally feeling better? Why would He take my friend, my confidant, my protector? I could not make sense of what was happening and why God was making my family suffer.

And yet—But God.

39

Over time, and through deep soul-searching and spiritual surrender, I realized something: My father's death was not about me. It was about his life journey and his relationship with God. One night, I woke up with a clarity I can only describe as divine. I felt God speak to my heart:

"His passing wasn't your punishment. It was My plan for him. He didn't want a lingering illness. He lived a full life, and he came home to Me."

That moment changed me.

If you're struggling with grief, especially while trying to hold onto your faith, here are a few things I've learned that may help:

1. It's Okay to Question God—He Can Handle It

Grief often brings up questions we've never dared to ask. Don't feel guilty for wrestling with your faith. God is not intimidated by your anger, confusion, or heartbreak. In fact, those raw emotions are exactly what God wants from you, your authentic self. Trust and believe God already knows you inside and outside and those emotions strengthen your relationship with Him.

2. Healing Isn't Linear—And That's Normal

You might have good days followed by days where the grief feels fresh all over again. That's okay. Healing isn't a straight path. Give yourself grace in the process.

3. Surround Yourself with Support, But Also Make Space for Solitude

Grief counseling, family, friends, and your faith community can be lifelines. But don't underestimate the power of being still—of sitting quietly with God, allowing Him to speak into your brokenness.

4. Look for God in the Small Moments

For me, it was a whispered word in the night. For you, it may be a song, a verse, a memory, or a stranger's kindness. God will meet you in the places you least expect, if you let Him.

5. Remember: Your Loved One's Story Was About More Than Just Their Death

My father's life had meaning, purpose, and impact. His passing was not the end of that legacy—it was its completion. Shifting my focus from my pain to God's purpose was what began to set me free.

6. Faith Doesn't Eliminate Grief—But It Does Redeem It
Psalm 30:5 says,

"Weeping may endure for a night, but joy comes in the morning."

I clung to that verse even when I didn't feel the joy. Now I understand that joy is not about being happy again. It's about the quiet assurance that God is still in control, even in the chaos.

Final Thoughts: Be Still and Let God Work

If you're grieving right now, I want to remind you that there is hope. You don't have to rush the process. You don't have to have all the answers. Stand still. Be quiet. Let God work on you. He will bring you through.

Isaiah 40:31 tells us,

"those who hope in the Lord will renew their strength. They

will soar on wings like eagles; they will run and not grown weary, they will walk and not faint." That's what God did for me.

Grief may change you, but it doesn't have to break you. And when you're ready, your story—like mine—can become a light for someone else walking through the darkness.

～

"Grief often brings up questions we've never dared to ask. Don't feel guilty for wrestling with your faith. God is not intimidated by your anger, confusion, or heartbreak."

Chapter Eleven
Don't Give Up On God
Dr. Shryl Whigham

I sat in my car in the parking lot outside the bank. I had just deposited my paycheck (this was some years before direct deposit) and was balancing my checkbook. I was worried that my deposit wouldn't cover the checks I had written the night before. (Yes—this was before online bill pay, too.) Somehow, by the grace of God, the deposit covered the checks, but left only a few dollars in my account, and it would be two weeks before my next paycheck. I felt a lump in my throat as tears began welling up in my eyes. Before I knew it, I was sobbing and shaking uncontrollably. What was I going to do? How was I going to make it? How did I even get to this point? I was ashamed. I was smarter than this. I don't remember how long I sat there crying and questioning myself, but at some point, I told myself to pull it together. I was on my lunch break, and I had to go back to work.

A little history...I graduated from college at age 21 with a bachelor's degree in radio, television, and film. The world was my oyster, or so I thought. I was smart and talented, and without a doubt, I would quickly find a job in my field. (Stick a pin in that bubble.) After a year of looking for a job in radio and television, I succumbed to a parental ultimatum to "find a job, and find one quick," so I took a job managing a record store. It wasn't the ideal job or the career path I imagined, but within three years, I was making a pretty good salary. I hadn't given up on a career in radio or television, but I was no longer a starry-eyed dreamer. That was until one day, when a friend from college, whom I hadn't seen since graduation, came into the record store. He was working at a small radio station in the area, and they were looking for a receptionist. I applied for the position and was hired. Goodbye, record store; hello, career in radio! One problem. When I accepted the job at the radio station, the salary was nearly half what I was making at the record store. At the time, I didn't care. I was going to be working at a radio station. And that is how I became broke girl sobbing in the parking lot.

Perhaps you may be wondering where God is in this story. For now, I'll say, He was working His plan. Jeremiah 29:11 "For I know the plans I have for you...plans to prosper you and not to harm you, plans to give you hope and a future." Back to the story...

I dried my tears and went back to the radio station that day. I took on evening work at the record store (life lesson: never burn bridges) and weekend hours at a gift store in the city. Yes, I was working three jobs, and it was challenging, but I was able to make ends meet. However, more importantly, it was at this point in my life that my relationship with God became personal. Although I had been raised in the church and was a baptized, born-again believer, it was at this point that I came to understand what it is to have a personal relationship with the Lord. It became God and me in communion and conversation every day—and that was life-changing, life-defining. I prayed about everything. My spiritual life evolved. My faith grew. I began to trust God for everything. But that's not the end of the story.

Some weeks later, I answered the phone at the radio station, and the call was for me. It turned out that the friend who had recommended me for the job at the radio station mentioned me to another friend who worked for a major broadcasting company. She was calling about an opening she had for an assistant. Plans to prosper you and not to harm you, plans to give you hope and a future. I accepted the interview opportunity, and although I thought it went well, I was not offered the position. I was disappointed, but to my surprise, not devastated. I knew that God had a plan to prosper me. About three months later, the woman from the broadcasting company called again to tell me that the person she had hired didn't work out. She offered me the position, and, of course, I took it! My career took off. A few years later, the woman who had hired me left to work for a competitor. The general manager called me to his office and asked me if I knew how to do her job. I enthusiastically replied, "Yes, of course, I do!" and he responded, "Then the job is yours." An impromptu, one-question interview. A promotion. A significant pay raise. Only God!

Since that time, I've had to make many life-altering, life-defining decisions. Decisions that included a significant career change that meant giving up a high-salaried position in broadcasting to go back to school and start over in another field. What was (and has been) different is that the guidance of the Holy Spirit made this decision. It's what happens when you are in sync with the plan God has for you. It probably doesn't or won't make sense to most people, but "My thoughts are nothing like your thoughts," says the Lord. "And my ways are far beyond anything you could imagine." (Isaiah 55:8-9, NLT)

There have been many ups and downs, and many prayers, since the 24-year-old sat crying in the car that day. What I've learned on the journey is that God hears me and He does answer prayer. But He doesn't answer most prayers immediately, although He does answer some instantly. And for me, as I am sure for all of us, there are prayers yet to be answered. But no matter how hopeless or how helpless you may feel, no matter how impossible the problem or situation may appear to be, God sees you. God hears you. Don't give up on God.

~

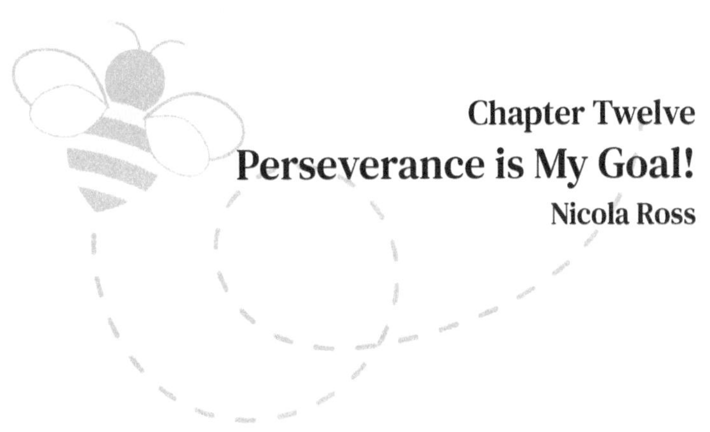

Chapter Twelve
Perseverance is My Goal!
Nicola Ross

"But those who wait on the Lord shall renew their strength; They shall mount up with wings like eagles, they shall run and not be weary, they shall walk and not faint." Isaiah 40:31 NKJV

When I observe people and listen to them speak, what matters most to me is their ability to communicate with truth and clarity. This allows me to reflect on myself and ask whether I am paying attention to my own truth and expectations. Taking mental notes and observing others can be a good way to evaluate the paths I want to pursue, but is everything I see meant for me? There's often confusion, contemplation, and certainty regarding the choices others have made in their lives. Will I make similar choices? Perhaps I will succeed where they struggled, or maybe I will encounter my own failures. Through life's highs and lows, we all experience some form of pain: whether it's being over-worked, settling down, raising children, attending school, or pursuing promotions. Regardless of what comes to mind, I believe that God has a way of guiding us toward our destiny in life.

What a transformative experience it was to speak about my journey! Attending college after high school was phenomenal. One of my older siblings had already gone to college, so it was my turn to embark on that adventure. I thought I knew the routine, so I was excited to be part of it too! I speak of this with genuine love and enthusiasm because my college years were truly special. I initially attended Monmouth College (now Monmouth University) for a brief period before transferring to Howard University in Washington, DC. I had a great experience at Monmouth, made wonderful friends, and began advocating for Black and Brown students, as I was one of them. However, I faced challenges with racism and personal relationships there, which prompted me to move on. My aspiration to attend a Historically Black College and University (HBCU) led me to Howard University, where I completed 3 1/2 years before transferring to another university closer to home with my kids, After graduating with my bachelor's degree. My life began to unfold for me, as I navigated my independence.

At Howard, I connected with church friends who introduced me to new families and relationships in DC. This was a significant part of my growth and understanding of how to build connections while navigating life. I must emphasize, "This was my way!" If we rely solely on our own understanding, we risk becoming entangled in life's thorns. Everyone has their own struggles, and some people carry heavier burdens than others.

During my college years, whether living in dorms or off-campus, I experienced both highs and lows. I faced setbacks, including failing expensive university classes, which taught me the importance of working and financing my own education. Stepping away from both God's guidance and my parents' support quickly introduced me to the concept of 'rock bottom.' Everyone's rock bottom is different, especially when you insist on doing things your own way.

In the year I was supposed to graduate from Howard University, I met a guy who quickly became my boyfriend. At around 21 years old, this relationship was new and exciting for me, and soon we decided to get married. Instead of focusing on my graduation that year, wedding planning took center stage. I got married at 24, and we stayed legally together for 18 years, during which time we welcomed three children into our lives.

Though I had built a family and paused my academic ambitions, after having my first child and taking three years off from school to be a new mom and wife, I decided to re-enroll. I returned to school as a part-time student while also working. After graduating, I got pregnant again, but this time I was determined to keep moving forward. In my sixth month of pregnancy with my second child, I enrolled in my first graduate class. After having my son, I enrolled full-time in graduate school. Juggling motherhood and academics felt chaotic at times, but I was determined to create meaningful friendships and connections for myself and my family. I realized I could no longer wait for others to reach out or stall my progress; I had to seize the moment and manage my time effectively.

Graduating with my Master's degree felt incredibly rewarding! However, it seemed that for some people, that achievement was insufficient. I faced constant questions like, "Why do you need all these degrees? Where will they lead you with small children at home? As a wife, shouldn't you be focusing on your marriage instead of your education?"

I was determined not to let these negative comments deter me. As a result, I sometimes strained relationships with certain family members and friends. Even when I felt the weight of separation from those close to me, I knew God was with me. I remained focused on my responsibilities to care for my family. Despite the challenges, I pressed on, striving for the things I wanted in life and what I thought my husband wanted too.

Did you recognize me saying the things "I" wanted again? I was trying to do all kinds of things to flourish my family by pursuing what "I" wanted us to do together. However, that wasn't how it was supposed to work; I just wanted to be the one making a difference with the support of my family. The real question should have been: Which family was I truly talking about? After several years, I realized that which I wanted wasn't what it was all about. Eventually, my marriage ended. We tried four times to make it work during our separation. We were together for 14 years and separated for four, which legally means it's been 18 years, right?

Once the big 'D' happened, nothing compared to the penetrating pain from your own family or loved ones. I dealt with the separation and divorce on my own for years. During that time, I remembered a saying I often heard: "When you're down or sick, you'll know who's in your corner!" It was a difficult period, and I could have used the support of the people I thought were friends and family. I initially thought I could handle it, and for a while, I did. I had some people I could talk to, but it wasn't the same as speaking with those who had a shared history with me. That made it rough, so I began to venture out again, but this time I had three little people to think about.

As time went on, my ex-husband and I struggled with decisions about who would keep our kids (as far as I was concerned, it should have been both of us). As long as we maintained communication between the two of us, we managed to co-parent. However, the physical distance between us and the cycle of arguing didn't help either. The full reality of separation was evident for both of us. This was definitely a new way of living, but I figured it out and persevered. Life was moving forward for me again. Even when I thought everybody else had forgotten me, I knew God hadn't. Perseverance meant more to me than anyone could understand. Having thorns in my life isn't easy, but as the Bible says, "God's grace is sufficient," and just as He has removed many thorns, He can also replace them with new ones. I continually boosted myself, reminding myself that I could get through this—and I did.

As a child, I always sensed that some things were different. My mother was overprotective and tried her best to watch over me, and I guess I learned that from her, as I became the same way with my children. My life was everything I wanted; of course, making mistakes was likely a result of me wanting to do things my way again. I often tried to remember how my mother did things to replicate her approach, although there were aspects I promised myself I wouldn't imitate. After giving birth to my first child, I would often tell my mom, these are newer times and a newer generation (I chuckle now because my kids tell me the same).

Anyway, things within my marriage continued to change—probably for the worse for me. Once the divorce was finalized and we had joint custody (with the kids living with their dad), I accepted that at the time. We communicated about parenting decisions until another blow came our way. Suddenly, I found myself responsible for paying child support, which was a shock.

The biggest shift in my perspective on life was understanding the importance of 'working together.' How can families build together without involving law officials or third parties in what we've created? For years, I felt angry and uncertain about whether my anger was directed at the world or the challenges it presented. Despite all the communication my ex and I had, I remained upset. Being the one assigned to pay anything, even with joint custody, was exhausting for me. I wanted to start a different kind of fight—not one with my ex, but a fight against the legal system that bases decisions on their own facts and the narratives told by lawyers. Whether accurate or not, the entire legal system operates as a cohesive group of supporters. Whatever happened to saving families? What about the feelings of the children? It was devastating to realize I would have to climb yet another mountain.

I suppose climbing a mountain is like: you win some, you lose some, but most of all, don't stop moving and clinging to God's unchanging word. I've been paying support for almost ten years now. The process has been challenging, but knowing that God sits on His throne and has never failed to help me with my bills gives me comfort. In light of God's blessings, He has orchestrated helpers—physically, emotionally, spiritually, and financially. As situations continued to change, I could feel God's presence through the people He sent my way, and I appreciate each of them. Even with moving around, changing jobs, and so forth, He has continued to keep me grounded. I don't know about anyone else, but this journey feels exhausting. However, proving myself to everyone remains my ongoing fight.

God is the only one who can manifest what He has in store for me. I have come to realize that I need to look at myself and adapt to the changes around me. Staying 'complete' is not an option; I must keep moving forward. I have to endure the pain of uncertainty and adjustment, knowing that I can remove my challenges one by one.

By placing your trust in God and focusing on Him, you can find success. He is the one who lets others witness what He has accomplished, not what I have done or what others believe they have achieved. Whether I have little or a lot, I will continue to remove the thorns, push through the pain, and persevere. That's my determination!

~

Chapter Thirteen

Abandoned to Abounding

Robin Hinton

"Daddy, why did you abandon me?"

It's a question that many children have asked or secretly wondered about. One day, while I was alone in my car, I heard this question seemingly come out of nowhere. I was startled and looked around to confirm that I was indeed alone. The question echoed again, "Daddy, why did you abandon me?" This time, I realized it was coming from within me, and a wave of anxiety washed over me, bringing tears to my eyes.

The question, "Daddy, why did 'You' abandon 'Me?'" was pointed and personal. Even though it originated from within, I didn't quite understand its significance. As I wrestled with feelings of wonder and unease, clarity began to surface through my tears. Remembering my experience as a 10-year-old, I realized I was crying out to my father, who had separated from our family: my mother, my sister, my brother, and me.

"What? God, are you kidding me? Now?"

Over four decades later, I was driving to pick up my father and stepmother to spend the entire day with them as they visited friends and family during their week-long vacation in Philadelphia. I see my father every year and have done so for the last 30 years. He was never abusive and fulfilled all his legal obligations towards us, yet I was in shock as I realized that a feeling I had buried deep inside me for 45 years—the little girl crying out for answers to feelings of abandonment—had resurfaced. "God, why now?" There are 52 weeks in a year, and I wished you had chosen one of the other 51 weeks so I could compose myself. With only 15 minutes left before I arrived, I felt puffy-eyed, red-faced, and unable to disguise my distress.

What else is hidden within me, God? I am afraid to confront what I don't know. This uncertainty is shaking my world because I thought I had healed from the divorce, but now I'm starting to question that. I don't like the idea of confronting the unknown parts of myself. "I don't know, God; only you do." Holy Spirit, please help me. As I sought comfort amidst my distress, the Spirit reassured me: "Trust your God. Don't rely on your own thoughts. He is God and will direct you. He's got you."

I spent the entire day in their company, driving between family visits. While at lunch and enjoying moments of pleasant conversation, my thoughts kept drifting back to that haunting question: "Daddy, why?" The car ride was enjoyable, but I remained preoccupied at a deeper level.

Following my father's guidance, we arrived at our next destination. After a warm welcome filled with hugs and greetings, I settled into a chair with a soda and snacks, and found myself looking at my dad. Suddenly, a process within my mind and heart revealed to me that he had not actually abandoned me. A memory surfaced— decades ago, I had heard my mother crying. I remembered walking into their bedroom, where she was packing my father's belongings into boxes. I kept asking, "Mommy, why are you crying? Why are you packing daddy's stuff?" At that moment, I had no understanding of the situation and I must have troubled her by following her as she carried the boxes outside.

Was she feeling abandoned too? I later learned that my parents had come to this painful agreement together. However, in the eyes of a young girl, the sense of abandonment took root deep within me, embedding itself in my soul. It became a sealed place that only God could unseal and expose.

"God, what kind of strategy is this for my healing?" I recalled Proverbs 3:5-6: "Trust in the LORD with all thine heart; and lean not unto thine own understanding. In all thy ways acknowledge him, and he shall direct thy paths." Who but God would drop such a revelation on me, immersing me in it for hours to heal the pain through discernment, love, and compassion? He had prepared me with trials and triumphs, experiences and failures, growth and setbacks, so that I would be resilient enough to fall into His arms and surrender to His care. I realized that my resilience was only found in Him.

God's help comes at His appointed time, and He chose that day and hour. Clearly, I was not ready to face this revelation in the prior 45 years for reasons I may never understand. While visiting various homes, sharing meals, and driving around, I recognized God's omniscience at work. He had revealed my inner truth, given me 15-20 minutes to sit with it, and then allowed me 8 hours to wrestle with it. Amazingly, He healed me before the day was over.

Had God revealed this two weeks prior, I would have been stuck laboring over it for those two weeks. If He had shown it to me after their visit, I might have spent months agonizing over thoughts, approaches, and resolutions. Instead, God loved me enough to immerse me in this challenging experience while surrounding me with His comfort through the Holy Spirit until all those questions became irrelevant. He taught me resilience in times of trouble, empowering me to trust Him, surrender to Him, and heal in His way.

I would not realize for many years that I was never truly alone or forsaken. From the moment my subconscious concealed my feelings of abandonment, God kept the child within me safe until I developed resilience. Throughout those years, the Holy Spirit encouraged me even when I was unaware of God's protection, helping to build that resilience. I was held until His appointed time, as my faith grew and I overcame obstacles in failed relationships, health concerns, financial challenges, and more. God was perfecting me through His love and power. Yes, He directed my path, and I acknowledge Him. In God, I was never unloved; I always had a Father who would never leave, forsake, or abandon me.

∽

"Who but God would drop such a revelation on me, immersing me in it for hours to heal the pain through discernment, love, and compassion! He had prepared me with trials and triumphs, experiences and failures, growth and setbacks, so that I would be resilient enough to fall into His arms and surrender to His care. I realized that my resilience was only found in Him."

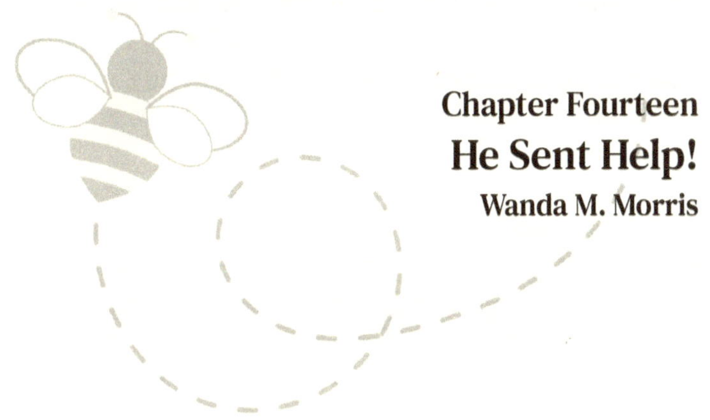

Chapter Fourteen
He Sent Help!
Wanda M. Morris

"God is our refuge and strength,
an ever-present help in trouble."
PSALM 46:1 NIV

Have you ever needed help but couldn't find it, no matter where you looked? Many of us would likely answer this question with a resounding "Yes." I ask this question as a reflection of my own experience growing up. As a child, I seldom asked for help because I felt that the people who should have been looking out for my well-being—my mom and dad—weren't always available. They were physically present but sometimes too preoccupied with their own challenges. I don't doubt that my parents loved us, and they did provide for us as a family unit, but that changed when they divorced during my early teen years.

Since I didn't trust that I would find help, I sought it on my own, and some of those avenues were unhealthy. By the age of thirteen, I was using drugs as a way to escape the sexual and physical abuse I was experiencing. I lived a life of promiscuity and became pregnant as a young adult.

I grew up in church, but I never trusted God, especially after He allowed my best friend to die—the very person I was depending on for rescue. My friend's death caused my heart to ache and led me to become angry with God to the point that I vowed never to step foot in a church again. Now, as a adult, I realize that God was extending His mercy.

As the years passed, I lived my life independent of God. I don't think I ever asked Him for anything. Over time, people in your life, transition. My grandmother passed away in 1985. I broke my vow and attended her service held in a church, but I don't recall praying. From 1985 to 1987, my family faced one tragedy after another. First, my grandmother, then two of my uncles, and finally my mother passed away. My mother succumbed to esophageal cancer three months before her 47th birthday. This devastation caused me to continue my downward spiral. I found myself in a toxic relationship, and my drug use increased. A part of me wanted to die.

During this time, I was the mother of two small children, ages 4 and 9. I received no emotional support from their father, so I stayed with my sister and her husband, hoping we could support one another in our grief. They had children of their own. Holding my 2-month-old nephew on my chest was my only comfort. I would hold him and sleep all day. I just wanted to die! My grief was unbearable. I started taking my mother's morphine, hoping for an early death. Since I wasn't able to take my life through self-medication, I finally sought help. I had two small children who needed their mother. Thank God for the other adults in the house who took care of their needs when I was incapacitated.

My abuse of pills and sleep continued for days until one day, while standing in my sister's kitchen, I heard a voice say, "Get yourself together! You know that no one will take care of your children the way you want them to." In that moment, my mind became clear. I stopped taking the medications, both mine and my mother's. I pulled myself together as best I could and took my children home.

I know without a doubt that it was God who spoke to me. However, He used a voice that was familiar to me—one I longed to hear: my mother's. Was this the end of my struggles with feeling alone or without help? Absolutely not, but it marked the beginning of my realization of where my help comes from.

I Corinthians 10:13 (NIV) states, "No temptation has overtaken you except what is common to mankind. And God is faithful; he will not let you be tempted beyond what you can bear. But when you are tempted, he will also provide a way out so that you can endure it."

God saved me by providing a way out. At first, I didn't understand this, but now it's clear to me. I had to learn where to look, whom to seek, and when to ask for help, and He was always there. God was listening, even when my soul cried out for assistance without me voicing it. He heard my silent plea and rescued me. God is my source of help. When I was truly saved, born-again, I realized that no one loves me like God does. No one will care for me in the same way He does, and I am so grateful that God sent help my way. And because God loves you, He will send help to you as well.

Let my story remind you that whenever you feel alone or without support, look up. God will send help. For many years, I searched for a savior in the flesh—my dad, my friend, and even my children's father—but none of them could truly help. Ultimately, God sent me the help I needed: Himself!

> *I lift up my eyes to the mountains—*
> *where does my help come from?*
> *My help comes from the Lord,*
> *the Maker of heaven and earth.*

PSALM 121:1-2 NIV

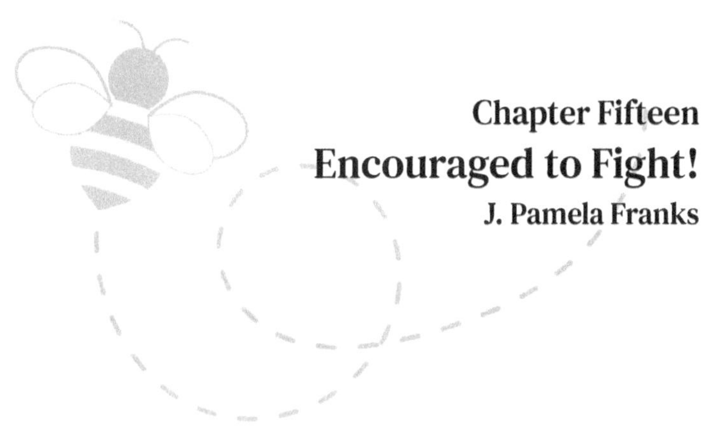

Chapter Fifteen
Encouraged to Fight!
J. Pamela Franks

"For a righteous *man* may fall seven times
And rise again..."
Proverbs 24:16 NKJV

I grabbed the remote to take a minute and do absolutely nothing! I perused the plethora of channels when the phone rang. Determined not to be disturbed, I pushed the do-not-disturb button. It was at that moment I heard the woman on television say, "All my life I had to fight." It was enough to stop me in my tracks. Sure enough, it was Sophia, played by Oprah Winfrey, in The Color Purple. As electrifying as her performance was, so were her words like electricity that invaded both the frontal and temporal lobes of my brain. I began to reflect on how many times in my life I had to fight.

When we think of fighting, we think of some confrontation or struggle to contend in battle. The Bible references physical battles, personal struggles, and spiritual warfare. We can all attest that we've had our share of fights in life.

As I reflect on childhood memories, I can recall the happiest day in my then seven years of life. My parents and I drove up to this big, beautiful single-family home. Beautifully landscaped with pink and white azaleas, big apple trees, which became a source of income during the school year, selling candied apples, and a backyard big enough for a horse to run. To me, it was the best house on the block because my parents had achieved the American dream of homeownership. I looked forward to meeting new friends and later discovered that the first friends I met were the neighborhood bullies.

I mainly stayed in the house after that discovery. However, every child wants to make friends. I learned of a private track club, so my parents allowed me to join after meeting with the coach. I shared with my mother that my schoolmates were bullying me, and that track would be a good way to meet new friends. Like any other African American (Black) mother, she gave strict instructions on how things worked. She explained that I should learn to defend myself and not allow anyone to beat me up. If I didn't, I could expect another whipping when I got home. Out of fear, those words became the laws that governed my childhood behavior.

I was excited to join the private track club called the Gazelles. Mr. Clark (track coach) encouraged me to be a winner. He told me I would be the next Wilma Rudolph, who faced many challenges. Born prematurely, diseased, and disabled. Against all odds, she became the first American Woman to win several Olympic gold medals in track and field at a single Olympic Games. She was the fuel that charged me up and got me running to win. I never missed a track practice or meet. One day, on the way to track practice, excited and proudly adorned in my blue and red Gazelle's track suit, with my spikes hanging over one shoulder attached by the shoestrings like the professional athletes, I felt empowered and looked the part.

I noticed behind me a group of girls chanting, "kick the bucket," and, to my surprise, wouldn't you know it, it was the neighborhood bullies. The chanting grew louder as I began to speed walk. All I could hear was my mom's voice saying, "Let somebody whip you and expect one when you get home." I felt a foot in my back and realized I was the bucket they were referring to. Like David, I had to encourage myself in the Lord and defeat the giant of fear. I rose to my feet, picked up my tarnished pride and track shoes with tears streaming down my face, and fought. I arrived at track practice and ran the track like the bullies were still chasing me. The victory was mine because they ran home bloody, battered, and bruised.

As time went on, my timeline of battles looked like an Egyptian hieroglyphic; a complex compilation of life's carvings that are difficult to understand. After High school graduation, I had plans to become a nurse, only to discover that my first year of college was interrupted by a beautiful impediment called mother-hood. So, my dreams of becoming a nurse became a lifelong reality: working full-time and raising children. Encouraged to rise like the little girl who had been knocked down, I grabbed hold of that bully called setback and won with the weapons of determination. In hindsight, out of that struggle came two beautiful, successful daughters — college graduates, one of whom owns three childcare centers and the other an Operating Room Charge Nurse — both of whom I am incredibly proud of.

Education and hard work became our recipe for success. The ones I encouraged to succeed became my inspiration to overcome any limitations and achieve more. So, I went back to school and received several degrees. My goal of achieving economic prosperity was met with denied promotional opportunities due to political cultures filled with people with lofty titles who lack intelligence and integrity.

I succeeded because I was encouraged to fight.

Even as a young child, my faith in God has always been strong. At ten years old, I heard the Preacher say, "If you hear the Lord calling run down these isles," and I did just that. I had gone to Church with my mom's good friend, and she came chasing after me, but the Preacher said, "hold on now, sister Lorraine, turn the baby loose." He asked if I had heard the Lord, and I answered, Yes; and I've been running for Jesus ever since. Fast forward to October 1999: the Lord called again. This time, I was afraid to answer the phone. It rang for six months until I said yes to the call to preach the gospel in March of 2000. I served as an itinerant minister until 2010 and then answered the call to the Pastorate. I became the Pastor of Spirit of Excellence Ministries. I needed direction, encouragement, and support, and the Lord provided. I came to realize that actual change isn't achieved through the influence of others, but through change in one's own mind and actions.

In 2020, I became a caregiver for my mom, who suffered a stroke. Her illness forced me to shift gears in ministry. The doctors said she was bleeding from the brain and advised us to make final arrangements; and if she made it through the night, she would never walk, eat, or talk. Psalm 30:5 says, "Weeping may endure for a night, but joy cometh in the morning." Shall I say that joy came in the morning, and to date, my mom is talking trash and eating chicken wings with the twist-and-turn method. What is the twist-and-turn method, you might ask? Put the wing in your mouth, twist it, and turn it; only the bone comes out. Did I also mention that she walks down the church aisle with the walker like Miss America? I hear y'all saying, "Won't He do it?" So be encouraged, you will have to fight, but your time is coming.

Scripture states, "For the race isn't given to the swift, nor the battle to the strong, nor bread to the wise, nor riches to men of intelligence and understanding, nor favor to men of ability, but time and chance overtakes them all." Ecclesiastes 9:11 AMP

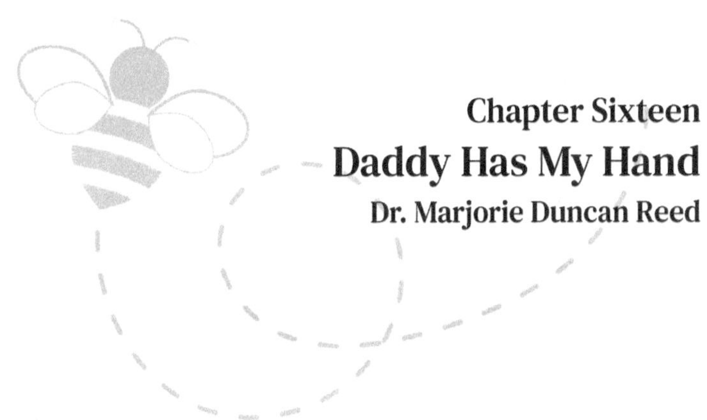

Chapter Sixteen
Daddy Has My Hand
Dr. Marjorie Duncan Reed

As soon as church is over, I'm going to Grandmom and Grandpop Duncan's house. As I left the church, Mommie watched me walk up the dirt road until it was time to make a left on Decatur Road. Daddy was at Grandmom and Grandpop's house, watching for me as I walked two more streets to get to the house. And all I have to do is say "how to do" to the older people sitting on their porches. That's what they called being respectful.

And then Daddy will be looking out the window, watching and waiting for me.

Opening up the white fence gate was so exciting to me. Because as soon as I got in the house, Grandpop wanted me to show and tell him how the different saints got happy in church and shouted.

Sis. Smith got happy and shouted, and I could mark her real good. He would then give me a dime. And then I would show him how Sis. Edith got happy. I really could shout like her. And that would be 15 cents. Oh, how he laughed.

Then, we would go to the backyard to feed the chickens. Walking past the well, which was a hole in the ground that was covered with boards, Grandpop always reminded me not to step on the boards; he watched me and stayed with me every step of the way. We would even pick some grapes off the vine.

Then Grandmom would call us to eat dinner. And I was always asked to say the grace to bless the food. I was so proud. Mommie had taught me to pray, and now, it was more people at the table who would hear me pray.

As it started to get dark, it was time for Daddy to take me home.

Daddy and I would have to walk to the trolley in Crestmont. That was a long walk. Dirt roads, wow, I hated it. We had to get to the next town called Ardsley. I hated that ride on the trolley; it was dark; you couldn't see out the windows, and the trolley made a lot of noise.

When we got off the trolley in Ardsley, we had to walk home. It was a long walk, but Daddy held my hand. Daddy was not a talker; we just walked quietly but fast. I skipped, walked, ran, and sometimes jumped to stay up with him. There were no sidewalks like today. We walked in the middle of the street. Potholes and puddles, uneven roads, but I never let go of Daddy's hand.

Sometimes, a few houses had their porch lights on, but that was not enough light for me. There were no streetlights. And very few cars were on the road in the neighborhood. And I didn't like it when the dogs would be barking. And their growling was even worse. They seemed so close.

I couldn't see where I was going, but Daddy could. He knew the road. When I stumbled, Daddy pulled on my hand to keep me from falling. And when I got tired, Daddy picked me up and carried me. I tucked my head on his shoulder, closed my eyes, sucked my thumb and went to sleep. All was well in Daddy's arms. I slept like a baby because Daddy knew the way to get me home.

One day I was thinking about my Daddy and our relationship. My Daddy was not a talker. What he said he meant, and what he meant he said. It was not up for discussion. Daddy loved me and made provisions for me, and all I had to do was obey him and trust him. And everything would be alright.

Well, one day, I was reading Psalm 73:23-24, and I saw my Daddy. Let me tell you what it says:

"Nevertheless I am continually with thee, thou hast holden me by my right hand. Thou shalt guide me with thy counsel, and afterward receive me to glory." WOW!

Daddy was with me all the way. HE WAS WITH ME, DO YOU HEAR ME? I didn't have to look for him; he was there all the time. He was always with me. No wonder I could walk, jump, skip, hop, walk in puddles of water, and keep up with him; it was because he was holding my hand. I never let go of his hand.

Just like God is holding my hand right now, with all that I am going through and have been through, my God was holding my hand. I was married for 35 years, lost my husband 25 years ago, had three children, and took care of elderly and sick parents and in-laws. God was holding my hand every step of the way. And, I do mean every "step."

And then He guided me with his counsel. WOW! All I had to do was listen to what he said. Daddy knows the road. He can see farther than I can see. He can hear all of the noises around me that frighten me. I need to let him guide me.

But let me tell you, as I look back on this now and see where I am today, All I can say is ONLY GOD! HE STILL HOLDS MY HAND! HE KNOWS THE WAY THAT I SHOULD TAKE.

There have been some dark days; I walked, skipped, hopped, and some days scared, but I kept my hand in His hand. There were days that He carried me, and I snuggled and fell asleep.

So excuse me, I feel a praise coming on.

Now I know why Sis Smith and Sis Edith's hands went up, and they started waving them in the air. Now I understand why they kept saying Glory Hallelujah. My feet can't stay still WHEN I THINK OF THE GOODNESS OF JESUS

Give me a minute; I got more than the 25 cents that Grandpop gave me to praise God for.

MY GOD IS STILL HOLDING MY HAND AND LEADING ME ON TO GLORY!

JUST HOLLER HALLELUJAH ONE TIME FOR ME!

~

"Just like God is holding my hand right now, with all that I am going through and have been through, my God was holding my hand."

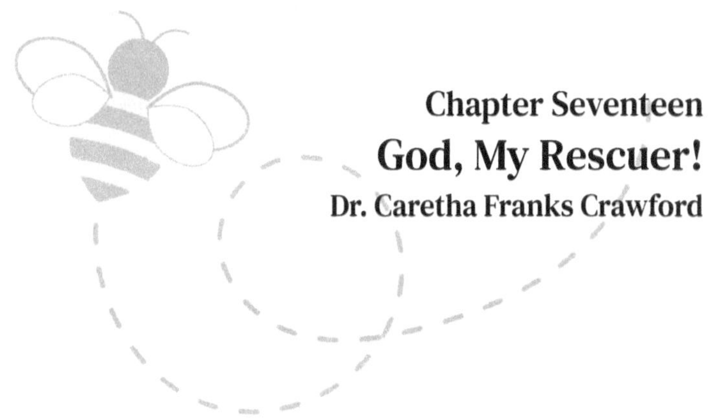

Chapter Seventeen
God, My Rescuer!
Dr. Caretha Franks Crawford

Throughout our lives, we acquire essential life skills through observation and practical training. These skills are not merely theoretical; they have real-world applications and can be pivotal in vulnerable or life-threatening situations. Common training scenarios include maintaining composure when faced with an aggressive dog, safely steering a vehicle that skids on ice, escaping from a sinking car, evacuating during a house fire, and assisting someone who is choking using CPR. Each of these situations demands quick decision-making. The question remains: will individuals recall their training and respond effectively during these crises, or will they succumb to panic or inaction?

I have encountered several of these challenges in my life. One incident that stands out vividly is a near-drowning experience I had at Bondi Beach while vacationing in Sydney, Australia, in December 2018. While enjoying one last splash in the ocean before traveling to another city, the rushing waves lifted me off my feet, leaving me immersed in water. Even though my instincts told me to fight physically for my life by thrashing in the water, my acquired knowledge urged me to stay calm, relax, and not struggle against the water. Surprisingly, I did just that; I remained calm. However, just when I thought I had finally regained control, another wave came and pushed me back underwater. It's important to note that I did not know how to swim. The thought running through my mind was, "I have to get up; I don't know if anyone knows that I am in trouble." Once I was out of danger, I learned that my husband had been rushing to my aid. Ultimately, it was God who saw me, subdued the waters, and rescued me. After what felt like hours, I finally stood on my feet with water around my calves, exhilarated to be free.

This experience caused an old back injury to resurface, and I needed Tylenol to relieve the pain. We quickly learned that there was no Tylenol available in Sydney. After some research, we found a chemist who recommended a similar drug that alleviated the pain in my back.

However, the emotional trauma from the incident was not as easy to soothe. I would relive the experience whenever I closed my eyes. The pounding of the water and my sense of helplessness washed over me like the waves of the ocean. Images of what happened and what could have happened haunted me for days.

God, and God alone, kept me calm and helped me resist panic. Yes, I had been taught to avoid fighting the water in such situations, but that's much easier said than done. The temptation to struggle was real, but it was God who gave me the strength to remain calm. The danger of drowning was imminent.

Of course, the enemy never misses an opportunity to exploit our vulnerability. Trauma opens the door for his attacks. Satan, the enemy of our souls, whispered in my ear, telling me things like, "Only two people were supposed to come back to the United States," referring to my husband and daughter. The sixteen-hour flight back to the States was a mix of gratitude and the enemy's taunts.

My near-drowning incident reassured me that God has the final word in every situation. He determines when and how we will meet Him in glory. The enemy sought to destroy me, but God demonstrated His mighty power over the forces of nature. He is faithful. This experience took my faith to new heights.

Sisters, at some point in life, you may find yourselves in a life-threatening situation. I pray that you will recall your training; if not, there is one thing you can always be sure of: The Almighty God will rescue you!

∼

"Even though my instincts told me to fight physically for my life by thrashing in the water, my acquired knowledge urged me to stay calm, relax, and not struggle against the water."

About the Author

Dr. Caretha Franks Crawford is a results-driven, ecumenical apostolic leader known for her spirit of excellence. She serves in various capacities: as a pastor, an international Bible teacher, an award-winning writer, a published author, and the Chief Administrative Officer of a worship school. Additionally, she is an entrepreneur, a dance minister, a writing coach, and the founder of multiple ministries aimed at encouraging, educating, equipping, and empowering God's people to fulfill their divine assignments.

In April 2023, Dr. Crawford was inducted into the Martin Luther King, Jr. Board of Preachers at Morehouse College in Atlanta, Georgia. She is the church planter of The Gateway to Wholeness Church Ministries in Largo, Maryland, and she has served as a Bible College and Seminary Associate Professor. Dr. Crawford is also a convener of numerous conferences, retreats, and seminars.

As part of the church's outreach, she established In Pursuit of His Presence Worship Arts Ministries, which caters to individuals seeking to pursue God's presence through the worship arts. Through this equipping school, affectionately known as IPHP, hundreds of dance ministers and worshippers have been trained and launched into higher levels of ministry. Thousands have attended the annual IPHP productions. Additionally, Dr. Crawford founded the Father's Table events to help those seeking healing from childhood wounds.

Dr. Crawford serves as a mentor through The R.E.A.L. Black Women in Ministry Thrive Initiative, a $1.5 million Lilly Grant mentoring program led by Dr. Suzan Johnson Cook and Pastor Brian Scott. She is also a founding member of the Global Black Women's Chamber of Commerce, which is also led by Ambassador Suzan Johnson Cook.

Dr. Crawford has preached across various denominational borders, inspiring and challenging both men and women through her dynamic teaching and preaching style throughout the United States and internationally in locations such as London, England; Sierra Leone, West Africa; Johannesburg, South Africa; and Braunwald and Zurich, Switzerland.

She has received numerous commendations and awards throughout her career. By God's grace and anointing, Dr. Crawford has published nine books, including *Dance: God's Gift to You; Hold On to Your Dream; Determined to Succeed; Relax and Receive; Jumpstart Your Mornings With Jesus; Promises and Prayers for Uncertain Times; Rebuild Your Life After Spiritual Identity Theft; Power for the Journey; and BEE Encouraged*. She is also a contributing author in *Soul Sisters* and *Rhythms of Rest,* both authored by Dr. Suzan Johnson Cook.

In 2019, Dr. Crawford established a publishing imprint for Christian independent authors called "SoAllMayKnow Publishing." Additionally, she is a blogger and a member of the Maryland Writers Association.

Dr. Crawford has further expanded her publishing company to include a magazine titled "Distinguished Woman," which highlights the accomplishments of women of color aged 60 and above. This magazine serves as a voice of encouragement for women to persevere with determination.

Before her current endeavors, Dr. Crawford worked as an Early Childhood Educator. She received her Bachelor of Science in Early Childhood Education from Winston-Salem State University in Winston-Salem, North Carolina. She earned both a Master of

Divinity and a Doctor of Ministry from Maple Springs Baptist Bible College and Seminary in Capitol Heights, Maryland.

In addition to her many accomplishments, Dr. Crawford is a greeting card designer and the former designer of educational children's clothing under the label Caretha's Kinder Creations. Her designs have been sold and exhibited in Paris, France (at the Salon International De La Mode Enfantine) and Puerto Rico. Locally, high-end boutiques and stores, including Bloomingdale's, carried her line. Caretha Crawford's "Clothes That Count" was highlighted in the Washington Post by the late fashion editor Nina Hyde. Her latest venture is a line of BEE Encouraged bling t-shirts.

Dr. Crawford is married to Rev. Clarence C. Crawford, and they have one grown daughter.

About Sherlene McIntosh

 **Sherlene McIntosh** is the proud daughter of the late Andy and Edna Jones, whom she lovingly describes as "the best parents in the world." She is a Rutgers University graduate with a bachelor's in political science and sociology and has done some graduate studies at George Washington University.

After more than three decades of dedicated service at the U.S. Department of Education, Washington, D.C., where she held various managerial roles, Sherlene retired as a seasoned public servant. She now serves as the Executive Assistant to Bishop Lynda Brown-Hall at Nevertheless Outreach Ministry Church in Washington, D.C. She also serves as the Community Outreach Lead, playing a key role in distributing Narcan kits and fentanyl strips, and providing educational resources to help prevent overdoses in the community.

Her love for God is profound, and her favorite scripture is Proverbs 3:5-6. She is also a Distinguished Toastmaster (DTM), with a passion for helping people find their voice, whether they are overcoming addiction or just finding their way in life. In her spare time, she loves to read and enjoy some jazz, and she treasures time spent with her two amazing adult sons, Jason and Matthew, whom she considers simply awesome and amazing.

About the Contributors

 **Dr. Michelle Boone-Thornton** is a transformational leader, international speaker, and World Civility Ambassador dedicated to empowering Black women to embrace authenticity and cultivate emotional resilience. As the founder of *Removing the Mask Coaching & Consulting* and author of the *Transforming Your Reality* book series, she helps women navigate the duality of public success and private struggles, guiding them toward true inner peace.

A sought-after educator, mentor, and advocate, Dr. Boone-Thornton specializes in emotional wellness, leadership development, and faith-based empowerment.

As a professor and industry leader in Human Services, Dr. Boone-Thornton prepares students across the world to advocate for social justice, provide compassionate care, and develop impactful solutions that uplift individuals and communities.

Her work extends beyond the classroom and consulting—she is a dedicated champion of global peace initiatives and community transformation, collaborating with leaders and organizations to create sustainable change.

Dr. Boone-Thornton's mission is rooted in empowering lives, celebrating leaders, and championing civility across continents.

Her Motto: "Unveiling authenticity, transforming lives, and empowering leaders across continents."

Follow her journey at **drmichelleboonethornton.com**.

Lakia Bradley. Born and raised in Maryland, Lakia Bradley is a devoted mother of three wonderful children and the cherished daughter of Barbara and David Adams, Jr., with her biological father being the late Gerald Stewart, Sr.. A gifted educator, she served as a teacher for 17 years, shaping young minds with compassion and purpose. Lakia is also a multi-talented entrepreneur whose creative abilities have birthed numerous projects and artistic ventures. In 2016, she answered her spiritual calling and was licensed as a minister at Enon Baptist Church. Through her faith, creativity, and resilience, Lakia continues to inspire and uplift everyone she encounters.

• Trailblazer • Visionary • Event Strategist • Master Networker • Event Producer Extraordinaire • Author • Speaker and Trainer

Theresa Royal Brown is the Event Producer Extraordinaire by trade, producing event experiences with excellence. Her passion is connecting people of all walks of life through networking. She accidentally fell into speaking and training when someone overheard her giving networking advice to a fellow conference attendee. Now she travels around the country teaching those in the business world the correct way to network to get more clients, a new job, or a contract. She is known as the "Master" Networker and has authored several books: "Keep Calm and Pivot" and Top Level Connections (30 Tips to Become A Master Networker) are two of her titles. Theresa also has a powerful testimony and strives to inspire others by sharing her story of overcoming a major life challenge, which almost led her to the brink of suicide. In her book, "Not Built to Break" (Becoming Resilient Through Life Challenges), she chronicles the struggles and triumphs on her entrepreneurial path and how she has overcome them. She is married to her partner in life and business, and the man she adores, Charles L. Brown, Jr.

For more information on Theresa, visit: theresaroyalbrown.com, epnetonline.com or premiereventsmanagement.com.

~

Beverly Claiborne, known as the "Divine Transformation Coach," is a dedicated Wife, Mother, Author, and Entrepreneur.

As a Christian author of Abiding in God's Word, Speaker, and "Divine Transformation Coach," Beverly inspires individuals to "Become Fearless with their Faith" and to be more fruitful on their life's journey.

Beverly grew up in Indianapolis, Indiana. She has been featured in Woman of Wealth Magazine as "A Woman Walking in Her Divine Purpose." In 2023, she was honored with the "R.E.A.L. Black Women in Ministry Leadership Award" for outstanding community service through her Abide Products line of Christian gifts and services, presented by Dr. Suzan Johnson Cook, a notable figure from the Obama Administration and the first African American female pastor of the Global Black Women of Chambers. In 2024, Beverly was featured in Today's Purpose

Woman's Magazine, which exclusively highlights Christian leaders walking in their purpose and power. Beverly is the author of three book and exclusive designer for the Abide Inspirational journals.

Beverly's passion for sharing God's message is evident in her online course, "Live Wise and Well in Christ" mentorship program, which creates pathways for more women to fulfill their calling. Her audience benefits greatly from her message of a loving, all-powerful God who transforms lives, whether they are struggling or believe they are doing well.

~

Reverend J. Pamela Franks is known for the Prophetic mantle and liberating call on her life. Her teaching and preaching are one that ministers healing, strength, encouragement and deliverance through the impartation of the Holy Spirit. She is the Pastor of Spirit of Excellence Ministries in Columbia, MD.; a certified Interior Designer by trade receiving her undergraduate Studies from Maryland Institute College of Art earning an associate of arts degree in Interior Design. Realigned for her purpose; She later earned a bachelor of science degree in theology, and a master of divinity from the University of Family Bible Institute College and Seminary. She holds a bachelors in business administration from Strayer University. In addition to her earned degrees, she is a certified Life Coach, Christian Counselor specializing in Temperament therapy and Pastoral counseling who enjoys spending time with family, traveling and reading.

~

Reverend Robin Hinton is an associate minister at Zion Baptist Church in Ambler, PA. She has led various ministries, including Women's Ministry, Nursing Home outreach, and Youth Ministry. With over four decades of experience in ministry, human resources, education, and organizational development, she has held leadership roles in several Baptist churches and contributed to numerous church, community, and professional organizations.

Her career includes work with both Fortune 100 corporations and non-profit organizations, where she has actively designed and led workshops, conferences, and diversity initiatives. As a founding partner of Ubuntu Organizational Services, Reverend Hinton consults with churches and schools, advocating for anti-human trafficking initiatives and lobbying for increased funding to support church-based programs.

Recently, she launched Breath A Fresh Air, a venture aimed at providing individuals and organizations with tools for personal and group transformation. Reverend Hinton holds a Master of Divinity and has degrees from United Lutheran Seminary and Palmer Theological Seminary. She is also a certified Registered Corporate Coach and has multiple additional certifications.

Devoted to her family, Reverend Hinton strives to let her light shine before others so that they may see God through her actions.

Rhonda Murphy Lindo is an Administrative Assistant/ Office Manager for prominent Internal Medicine doctors in Washington, DC. She has over 39 years of experience in the healthcare field. It's a fascinating, busy, and very complex position, as she deals with a diverse range of patients. Rhonda ensures that every patient is treated with a professional and positive attitude, kindness, patience, and a smile. Her motto is "treat people as you want to be treated because you never know what a patient is going through."

Outside of work, Rhonda is an active member at John Wesley AME Zion Church in Washington, DC. She is involved in many ministries, but her passion lies in working with the Sunday School and serving as the Director of the Performing Arts and Liturgical Dance Ministry. Rhonda is a family girl and loves her family very much. Along with her siblings, her parents instilled in her a firm foundation in the Lord. Her mother's motto, which she pressed upon us to never forget, was "God comes first in all you do, and you can't live without Him."

God has blessed Rhonda with a wonderful and supportive husband, two amazing young adult children, and, most recently, a beautiful daughter in love. Rhonda is humbled and honored to have been invited by Dr. Caretha Crawford to be a part of such an amazing and spiritually inspiring publication.

~

Wanda M. Morris was born and raised in Washington, D. C., and now resides in Charles County, Maryland. She has been married for 32 years, a mother of 2, grandmother of 4, and a great-grandmother of 1. She retired as a ParaProfessional of the Prince George's County Public School System after studying and working in the field of early childhood education since 1992. Wanda has been an overcomer of drug addiction for over 30 years. And she loves being a faithful witness of God's delivering power. Wanda serves as a member of New Birth Christian Church in Suitland, Maryland, under the leadership of Senior Pastor Daniel Duncan and Pastor Emeritus LaVida Sistrunk.

∾

Hewlette Pearson is committed to excellence in teaching, motivating, and preaching the Gospel, she holds master's degrees in education (Johns Hopkins University) and divinity (Regent University).

For over 15 years, Hewlette taught job readiness, character development, and life skills to incarcerated individuals and returning citizens. She is the founder and president of iLove Now, Inc., a nonprofit promoting love through humanitarian programs in inner-city communities.

She has authored three impactful books: *The View from the Mountain*, *The Most Important Word* (foreword by Andraé Crouch), and *Get Got: Empowerment for Every Day Life Successes.*

∾

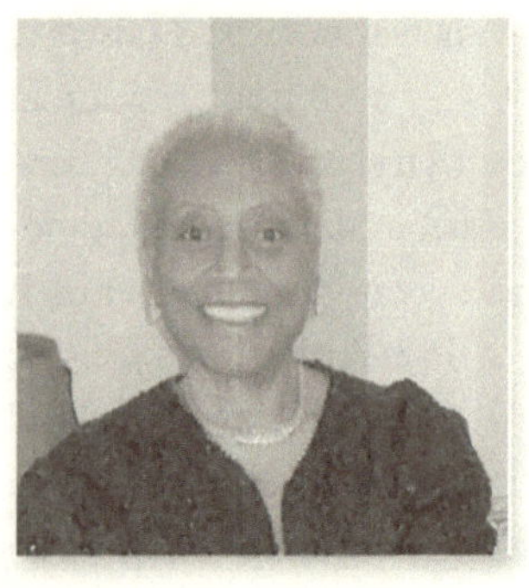

Rev. Dr. Marjorie Duncan Reed holds a master of theology and a doctor of ministry from Slidell Baptist Seminary in Louisiana. She is a retired pastor of St. Paul's Baptist Church in Conshohocken, Pennsylvania, a member of the Board of Preachers of the Martin Luther King Jr. International College of Ministers & Laity, and the first woman to serve as moderator of the 102-year-old Suburban Baptist Association of Southeastern Pennsylvania. She was the first African American Woman to serve as Chairman of the Board for the Merck Sharp & Dohme Federal Credit Union.

~

Judy Ann Reid is a retired U.S. military veteran who honorably served her country for 27 years. Her dedication and leadership left a lasting impact on those she served alongside. Following her military career, she embraced her spiritual calling, becoming an ordained Reverend and Prophetess. Judy holds a Bachelor's degree in Psychology, which deepens her understanding and compassion for others. Her life reflects unwavering faith, strength, and service —both in uniform and in ministry. Committed to uplifting others through guidance and prayer, Judy continues to inspire with her resilience, wisdom, and enduring dedication to both God and country.

~

Nicola Ross is a native of New Jersey. She enjoyed growing up in the place that she calls home. Nicola has been a Special Educator for 23 years, and has consistently advocated for individuals with autism. She is committed to "Union Representation for Teachers," an organization of educators who devote their time, energy, and passion to ensuring that children and young adults with autism can communicate for themselves and navigate the transitions of growing to the next level. Nicola is a co-author of "Autism Relationships Matters," alongside other authors who have children with autism. Nicola learned to push through pain and persevere, which allows her to help others do the same. She reminds others that it may be difficult, but how will you ever know the benefits of your efforts if you don't allow God to use you!

~

Carolyn P. C. Simms is a widow and mother of one grown daughter, and two grandsons. She is a native of Greensboro, North Carolina, and a graduate of Winston-Salem State University with a major in History. Carolyn is a retired teacher who still enjoys nurturing and serving in the community at 75 years of age. She is a certified Caregiver's Ambassador who works tirelessly encouraging widow's and children in her community and church, Sharpe Road Church of Christ in Greensboro, NC. She enjoys writing, reading and singing.

~

Tonya Sinclair Swindell is an occupational therapist, writer, poet, and featured columnist for the Suffolk News-Herald and New Journal and Guide. Tonya's writings have also been highlighted in Occupational Therapy Practice Magazine, "Determined To Succeed," by Dr. Caretha Crawford, and a documentary by McAfee Tech titled, "Why Millennials Are Leaving The Black Church." Tonya is from New Bern, North Carolina. She obtained a B.S. degree in Occupational Therapy (OT) from Medical University of South Carolina and a M.S. degree in Community Health Education and Health Promotion from Old Dominion University. She currently works with military veterans, helping them achieve greater independence and more fulfilling lifestyles. Tonya is a founding board member and active participant at Hesed Place, a 501 (c) (3) nonprofit serving adult survivors of complex trauma. She is currently a board member of United to Serve Outreach, a nonprofit dedicated to serving and enriching the Hampton Roads community. Tonya is a wife and mother of four teenage children. She enjoys watching live performances, visiting art museums, and exploring other cultures through food, travel, and learning new languages. Tonya can be reached at: Teacherwithapen@gmail.com or on Facebook at: Tonya Sinclair Swindell - Teacher With A Pen.

 **Dr. Shryl Whigham** holds a PhD in General Psychology from Walden University. She is a licensed clinical counselor and a certified clinical trauma professional. She has over 25 years of experience in behavioral health services, public health, and program management. Dr. Whigham specializes in mental health, trauma, and addictions treatment, clinical supervision, and grant management. She is a powerful force in the workplace and uses her positive attitude and tireless energy to encourage and train others.

Dr. Whigham is the Minister of Music and Creative Arts at Mount Airy Baptist Church in Washington, DC. She is a dance minister and a graduate of *In Pursuit of His Presence*. Dr. Whigham believes the best advice she ever received was to "stay on the journey with God." Among her favorite scriptures is 1 Thessalonians 5, verses 16-17: "Always be joyful. Never stop praying."

Contact the Author

FOR MORE INFORMATION about Dr. Caretha Crawford, her speaking and products, please contact:

Caretha Crawford Ministries International
PO Box 6718
Largo, MD. 20792
www.drcarethacrawford.com

For speaking engagements e-mail:
drcaretha.crawford@gmail.com

More Inspirational & Educational Books
by Caretha Crawford

978-1-7347064-8-2

978-1-7347064-6-8

978-1-7347064-3-7

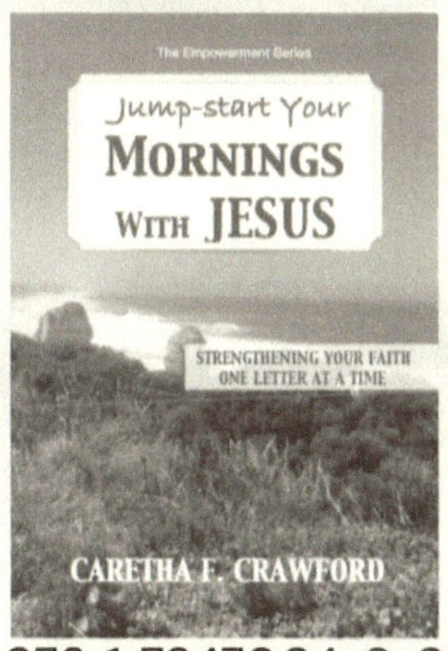

978-1-7347064-0-6

More Inspirational & Educational Books
by Caretha Crawford

978-1-5456-3449-3

978-1-49846-951-7

978-1-62136-688-1

978-1-61215-493-0